Excel® 2019
VLOOKUP
The Step-By-Step Guide

C.J. Benton

ISBN: 9781080007981

Thank you!

Thank you for purchasing and reading this book! **_Your_**
feedback is valued and appreciated. Please take a few
minutes and leave a review.

More books by this author:

For a complete list please visit us at:
https://bentonbooks.wixsite.com/bentonbooks/buy-books

- Excel Pivot Tables & Introduction To Dashboards The Step-By-Step Guide *(version 2016)*
- Excel 2016 The 30 Most Common Formulas & Features - The Step-By-Step Guide
- Excel 2016 The VLOOKUP Formula in 30 Minutes The Step-By-Step Guide
- Excel Macros & VBA For Business Users - A Beginners Guide

Questions, comments?
Please contact us at:

Email: bentontrainingbooks@gmail.com
Website: https://bentonbooks.wixsite.com/bentonbooks

TABLE OF CONTENTS

This book can be used as a tutorial or quick reference guide. It is intended for users who are comfortable with the fundamentals of Microsoft® Excel® and want to build upon this skill by learning the very useful VLOOKUP functionality.

While this book is intended for beginners, it does assume you already know how to create, open, save, and modify an Excel® workbook and have a general familiarity with the Excel® Ribbon (toolbar).

All of the examples in this book use **Microsoft® Excel® 2019**, however most of the functionality can be applied with Microsoft® Excel® version 2016. All screenshots use **Microsoft® Excel® 2019**, functionality and display will be slightly different if using **Excel® 2016**.

Please always **back-up your work** and **save often**. A good best practice when attempting any new functionality is to **create a copy of the original spreadsheet** and implement your changes on the copied spreadsheet. Should anything go wrong, you then have the original spreadsheet to fall back on. Please see the diagram below.

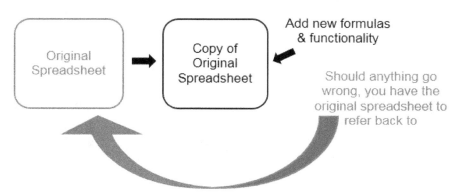

FILES FOR EXERCISES

The exercise files used in this book are available for download at the following website:

https://bentontrainingbook.wixsite.com/bentonbooks/excel-2019

Each chapter contains one or more examples in the below layout with step-by-step instructions.

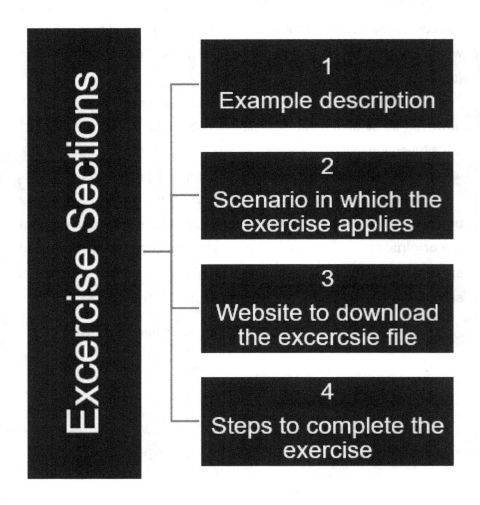

The below table is a summary of the functionality and features detailed in each chapter:

CHAPTER	FUNCTIONALITY
Chapter 2 VLOOKUP Introduction	▪ What the VLOOKUP formula does ▪ The parts of a VLOOKUP formula ▪ Two detailed examples with screenshots using a basic VLOOKUP formula
Chapter 3 Managing error messages	▪ How to avoid receiving error messages (#N/A, #REF, #VALUE! etc.) by incorporating IFERROR functionality into your VLOOKUP formula
Chapter 4 Extending the VLOOKUP Functionality	How to address the most common challenges when using the VLOOKUP function, such as: ▪ What to do when you attempt to lookup a value in the Table_array, but none exists ▪ What to do when you don't have a unique Lookup_value ▪ How using the INDEX & MATCH functions can be a viable alternative ▪ What to do when the Lookup_value is listed more than once in the Table_array
Chapter 5 Categories & Calculations	Applying the VLOOKUP to real-world situations: ▪ Using the VLOOKUP to *categorize* and *group data* based on specific criteria ▪ Using the VLOOKUP to *evaluate* and *calculate* an amount based on specific criteria
Chapter 6 Non exact VLOOKUP matching	▪ How to use the VLOOKUP in combination with the CONCAT and Wildcard functionality as an option when an exact match is not available

CHAPTER	FUNCTIONALITY
Chapter 7 Using The VLOOKUP across multiple workbooks	▪ Detailed example with screenshots of how to apply the VLOOKUP formula across *multiple* workbooks and tabs
Chapter 8 Troubleshooting	▪ A review of the five most common VLOOKUP error messages and issues and how to resolve them

WHAT IS THE VLOOKUP?

The VLOOKUP is an Excel® function allowing you to vertically search for a value from one Excel® list and return that specific value to a new Excel® list, based on a *matching lookup value*.

The VLOOKUP can be used on its own or in combination with other functions to extend its capabilities.

Conceptual Example:

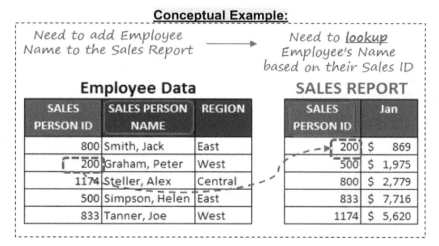

Syntax Example:

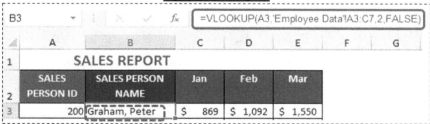

```
Syntax:
VLOOKUP (Lookup_value, Table_array, Col_index_num,
[Range_lookup])

All parameters are required, except for [Range_lookup]
```

THE 4 - PARTS OF A VLOOKUP (EXPLAINED)

❶ lookup value *(field to match)*:

The value you want to find (match) typically located in another worksheet or workbook.

In the below example, cell **'A2'** on **'Sheet1'** is selected, which has the Sales Person ID value of **'200'**. We will look to match this value in the worksheet labeled **'Sheet2'**. *Sales Person Name* is the value we want to lookup and *be returned* to the tab labeled **'Sheet1'**.

❷ Table array *(where to search)*:

The spreadsheet and range of cells searched for the ❶ Lookup_value. The field you want to match *must be* in the *first column* of the range of cells you specify in the ❷ Table_array.

In the below example, we're searching the tab labeled **'Sheet2'** with the cell range of **'A2:B6'**.

❸ Col index num *(what you want returned)*:

Is the column containing the value you want returned.

In the below example, column **'2'** of the tab labeled **'Sheet2'** contains the value of Sales Person Name which we want returned to the tab labeled **'Sheet1'**.

❹ Range lookup:

Is the optional value of **'TRUE'** or **'FALSE'**. The value of **'FALSE'** would return an *exact* match, while **'TRUE'** would return an *approximate* match.

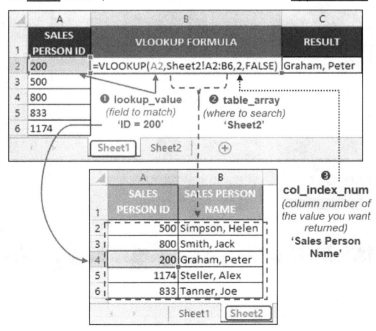

EXAMPLE 1: HOW-TO-APPLY A BASIC VLOOKUP FUNCTION

Scenario:

You've been asked to provide a list of first quarter sales by month for each sales person. You run a query from the sales database and generate an Excel® report. Unfortunately, the database only contains the sales person's ID, *but not their name*. You apply a VLOOKUP formula to return the Sales Person's Name from an existing Excel® spreadsheet to the new sales report.

WEB ADDRESS & FILE NAME FOR EXERCISE:
https://bentonbooks.wixsite.com/bentonbooks/excel-2019
Example_1_Basic_Vlookup.xlsx

Steps To Complete The Exercise:

Sample data:

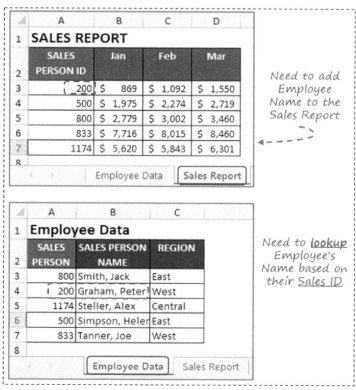

1. Open the Example_1_Basic_Vlookup.xlsx spreadsheet
2. Select the tab named **'Sales Report'**

3. Place your cursor in cell **'B3'**
4. From the Ribbon select **Formulas : Lookup & Reference**
5. From the drop-down list, select the option **'VLOOKUP'**

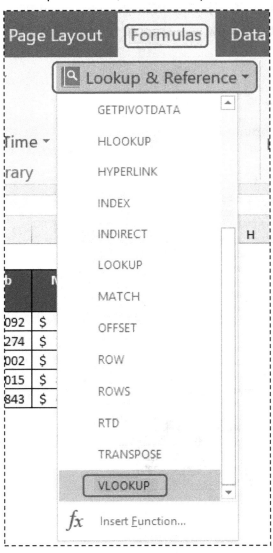

6. In the Function Arguments dialogue box enter the following:

    a. Click cell '**A3**' or enter **A3** in the dialogue box for the '**Lookup_value**' *(the sales person ID is the field we'll lookup on the 'Employee Data' tab)*

    b. For '**Table_array**', click on the tab '**Employee Data**' and select cells '**A3:C7**' *(this is the range of cells we're searching)*

    c. Enter the number **2** for '**Col_index_num**' *(this is the column number containing the sales person's name)*

    d. For '**Range_lookup**' enter **FALSE**

7. Click the '**OK**' button

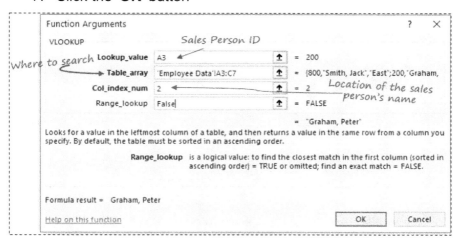

The following result should now be displayed on the **Sales Report** worksheet:

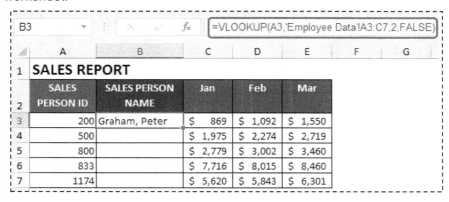

8. We need to do one additional step before we can copy this formula down to cells '**B4:B7**', we must add the U.S. dollar symbol **$** to the '**Table_array**'. This will prevent our cell range *(Table_array)* from changing:

↓↓ ↓↓

=VLOOKUP(A3,'Employee Data'!$A$3:$C$7,2,FALSE)

If we attempted to copy the VLOOKUP formula to cells '**B4:B7**' without adding the **$**, the result would be as follows, ***NOTE:*** *how the* '***Table_array***' *cell range changes:*

⊿	A	B	
1	**SALES REPORT**		
2	**SALES PERSO**	**SALES PERSON NAME**	
3	200	=VLOOKUP(A3,'Employee Data'!A3:C7,2,FALSE)	*Table_array*
4	500	=VLOOKUP(A4,'Employee Data'!A4:C8,2,FALSE)	*changes*
5	800	=VLOOKUP(A5,'Employee Data'!A5:C9,2,FALSE)	
6	833	=VLOOKUP(A6,'Employee Data'!A6:C10,2,FALSE)	
7	1174	=VLOOKUP(A7,'Employee Data'!A7:C11,2,FALSE)	

We would also receive a **#N/A** error in cells '**B5**' & '**B7**'

⊿	A	B	C	D	E
1	**SALES REPORT**				
2	**SALES PERSON ID**	**SALES PERSON NAME**	**Jan**	**Feb**	**Mar**
3	200	Graham, Peter	$ 869	$ 1,092	$ 1,550
4	500	Simpson, Helen	$ 1,975	$ 2,274	$ 2,719
5	800	#N/A	$ 2,779	$ 3,002	$ 3,460
6	833	Tanner, Joe	$ 7,716	$ 8,015	$ 8,460
7	1174	#N/A	$ 5,620	$ 5,843	$ 6,301

9. Copy and paste the VLOOKUP formula to cells '**B4:B7**'

=VLOOKUP(A3,'Employee Data'!$A$3:$C$7,2,FALSE)

⬛	A	B	C	D	E
1	**SALES REPORT**				
2	**SALES PERSON ID**	**SALES PERSON NAME**	**Jan**	**Feb**	**Mar**
3	200	Graham, Peter	$ 869	$ 1,092	$ 1,550
4	500	Simpson, Helen	$ 1,975	$ 2,274	$ 2,719
5	800	Smith, Jack	$ 2,779	$ 3,002	$ 3,460
6	833	Tanner, Joe	$ 7,716	$ 8,015	$ 8,460
7	1174	Steller, Alex	$ 5,620	$ 5,843	$ 6,301

⬛	A	B	C	D	E
1	**SALES REPORT**				
2	**SALES PERSON ID**	**SALES PERSON NAME**	**Jan**	**Feb**	**Mar**
3	200	=VLOOKUP(A3,'Employee Data'!$A$3:$C$7,2,FALSE)	869	1092	1550
4	500	=VLOOKUP(A4,'Employee Data'!$A$3:$C$7,2,FALSE)	1975	2274	2719
5	800	=VLOOKUP(A5,'Employee Data'!$A$3:$C$7,2,FALSE)	2779	3002	3460
6	833	=VLOOKUP(A6,'Employee Data'!$A$3:$C$7,2,FALSE)	7715.9	8014.9	8459.9
7	1174	=VLOOKUP(A7,'Employee Data'!$A$3:$C$7,2,FALSE)	5620	5843	6301

We have successfully looked-up and added the Sales Person Name to the quarterly sales report. We can now provide a list of the first quarter sales by month for each sales person.

Alternatively, for the **'Table_array'**, instead entering the range of cells (Employee Data!$A$3:$C$7) and having to add the $ to hold the array constant, you may enter the entire column **A:C** (Employee Data !A:C), provided the *entire column* contains only the data you want returned. This would eliminate the need to complete **step 8**.

However, depending on the number of records you're looking up *(the size of your data)*, there could be a reduction in performance speed when selecting the entire column. Especially, when *combining* the VLOOKUP with other functions as we will explore in the ensuing chapters. Please see the below screenshots for a complete example using entire the column instead of a cell range:

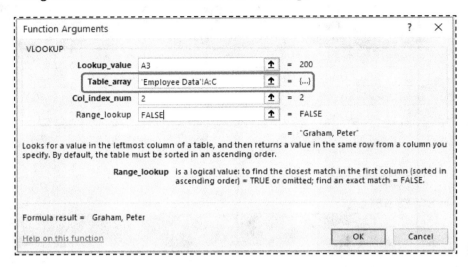

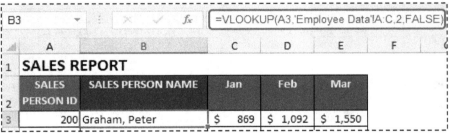

EXAMPLE 2: HOW-TO-APPLY A VLOOKUP USING THE ENTIRE COLUMN

Scenario:

You've now been asked to include the **sales region** to the list of first quarter sales by month, for each sales person.

WEB ADDRESS & FILE NAME FOR EXERCISE:
https://bentonbooks.wixsite.com/bentonbooks/excel-2019
Example_2_Basic_Vlookup.xlsx

Steps To Complete The Exercise:

Sample data:

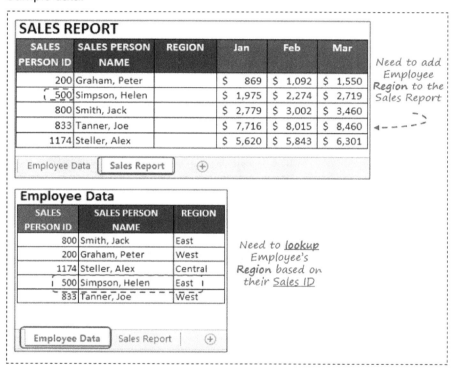

1. Open the Example_2_Basic_Vlookup.xlsx spreadsheet
2. Select the tab named '**Sales Report**'

3. Place your cursor in cell '**C3**'
4. From the Ribbon select **Formulas : Lookup & Reference**

5. From the drop-down list, select the option **'VLOOKUP'**

In the Function Arguments dialogue box enter the following:

a. Click cell **'A3'** or enter **A3** in the dialogue box for the **'Lookup_value'** *(the sales person ID is the field we'll lookup on the 'Employee Data' tab)*

b. For **'Table_array'**, click on the tab **'Employee Data'** and select **columns 'A:C'** *(this is the range of cells we're searching)*

c. Enter the number **3** for **'Col_index_num'** *(this is the column containing the sales person's region)*

d. For **'Range_lookup'** enter **FALSE**

6. Click the **'OK'** button

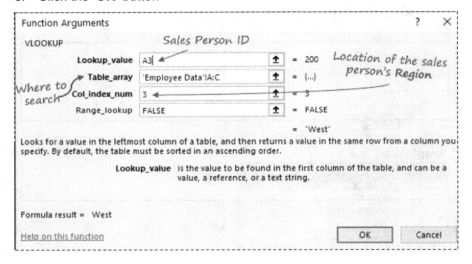

The following should be the result:

C3				f_x	=VLOOKUP(A3,'Employee Data'!A:C,3,FALSE)

	A	B	C	D	E	F
1	**SALES REPORT**					
2	**SALES PERSON ID**	**SALES PERSON NAME**	**REGION**	**Jan**	**Feb**	**Mar**
3	200	Graham, Peter	West	$ 869	$ 1,092	$ 1,550
4	500	Simpson, Helen		$ 1,975	$ 2,274	$ 2,719
5	800	Smith, Jack		$ 2,779	$ 3,002	$ 3,460
6	833	Tanner, Joe		$ 7,716	$ 8,015	$ 8,460
7	1174	Steller, Alex		$ 5,620	$ 5,843	$ 6,301

7. Copy and paste this formula down to cells '**C4:C7**'

The following should be the result:

	A	B	C	D	E	F
	SALES PERS	SALES PERSON NAME	REGION	Jan	Feb	Mar
1						
2	200	Graham, Peter	West	$ 869	$ 1,092	$ 1,550
3	500	Simpson, Helen	East	$ 1,975	$ 2,274	$ 2,719
4	800	Smith, Jack	East	$ 2,779	$ 3,002	$ 3,460
5	833	Tanner, Joe	West	$ 7,716	$ 8,015	$ 8,460
6	1174	Steller, Alex	Central	$ 5,620	$ 5,843	$ 6,301

We have successfully looked-up and added the Sales Person's **Region** to the quarterly sales report.

PUBLISHING VLOOKUP RESULTS

When sending the results of a VLOOKUP function to a customer or a co-worker, a common mistake is including the VLOOKUP formula in the spreadsheet, rather than pasting the results as a value. This is a very easy thing to do, but depending on where the **Table_array** worksheet or workbook is located can cause the following to happen.

In the example above, after adding the Sales Person Name & Region you:

- Deleted the worksheet, 'Employee Data', because you no longer needed the information
- Saved the workbook without noticing the VLOOKUP function is now broken
- Emailed the report to a customer

When the customer opened the spreadsheet, they likely would see an error in the results:

	A	B	C	D	E	F
1	**SALES REPORT**					
2	SALES PERSON ID	SALES PERSON NAME	REGION	Jan	Feb	Mar
3	200	#REF!	#REF!	$ 869	$ 1,092	$ 1,550
4	500	#REF!	#REF!	$ 1,975	$ 2,274	$ 2,719
5	800	#REF!	#REF!	$ 2,779	$ 3,002	$ 3,460
6	833	#REF!	#REF!	$ 7,716	$ 8,015	$ 8,460
7	1174	#REF!	#REF!	$ 5,620	$ 5,843	$ 6,301

Another common occurrence, if the **Table_array** was located in a *separate workbook*.

- You saved the workbook without issue
- You emailed the report to a co-worker
- When your colleague opens the spreadsheet, they likely would see a **!SECURITY WARING** message about the *file being linked to another workbook*:

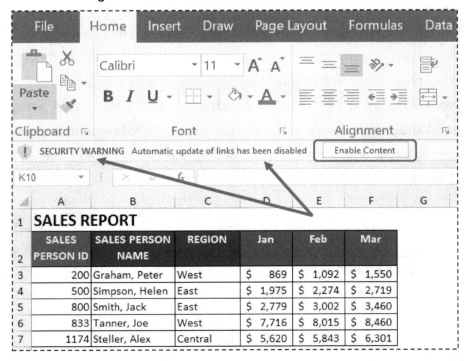

- If they clicked the **'Enable Content'** button, they may receive the following message:

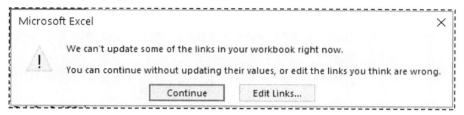

In either scenario, it could cause confusion, rework, or even lead a customer to have questions about you or the company you represent.

One of the easiest ways to address this issue is to **simply paste your VLOOKUP results as a value**. In the example above, we would:

1. Select (highlight) cells '**B3:C7**'
2. Click the '**Copy**' button or press **CTL+C** from your keyboard
3. Select the '**Home**' tab

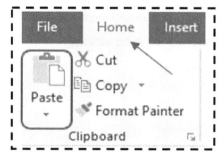

4. From the '**Paste**' drop-down menu select **'Paste Values'**
5. Select the **'123'** option

Please see image on the next page:

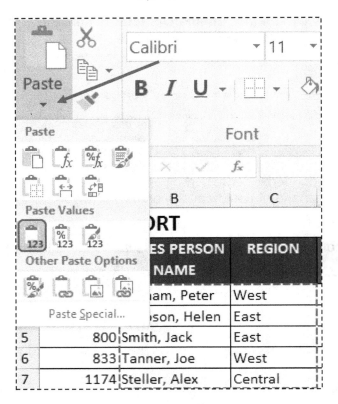

The VLOOKUP results are intact without any risk of error when you send them to a customer or a co-worker.

Next, we'll examine what to do when you attempt to lookup a value in the **Table_array**, but the value does not exist. Specifically, how to handle receiving the #N/A error message in your result set.

While the VLOOKUP formula is quite effective on its own, to fully harness it's capability we must *combine* it with other functions.

Before continuing, let's quickly review three additional functions needed to extend the VLOOKUP functionality. If you're already familiar with the **IF**, **Nested IF**, & **IFERROR** formulas, please continue to Example 3, page 22.

FUNCTION	DEFINITION
IF	IF formulas allow you test conditions and return one value *if true* and another *if false*
NESTED IF	NESTED IF formulas allow you test conditions and return one value *if true* and another *if false* **based on certain criteria**.
IFERROR	IFERROR returns a value you specify if a function *(in our case the VLOOKUP formula)* evaluates an error such as: #N/A #VALUE! #REF! #DIV/0! #NUM! #NAME? #NULL! **Otherwise** IFERROR **will return the result** of the *(VLOOKUP)* formula

IF FUNCTION

IF Syntax:

IF(logical_test, value_if_true, [value_if_false])

logic_test required, **value_if_true** required, **value_if_false** optional

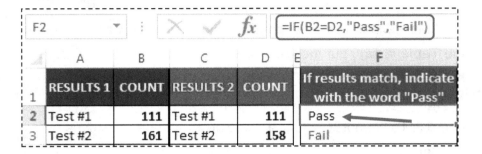

| F2 | ▼ | : | ✕ | ✓ | *fx* | =IF(B2=D2,"Pass","Fail") |

	A	B	C	D	E	F
1	RESULTS 1	COUNT	RESULTS 2	COUNT		If results match, indicate with the word "Pass"
2	Test #1	111	Test #1	111		Pass ←
3	Test #2	161	Test #2	158		Fail

NESTED IF

| F4 | ▼ | : | ✕ | ✓ | *fx* | =IF(B4=D4,"Pass",IF(B4-D4>5,"BIG FAIL","Fail")) |

	A	B	C	D	E	F
1	RESULTS 1	COUNT	RESULTS 2	COUNT		IF results match = **Pass** IF results DO NOT match = **Fail** IF results DO NOT match and the difference is greater than 5 = **BIG FAIL**
2	Test #1	111	Test #1	111		Pass
3	Test #2	161	Test #2	158		Fail
4	Test #3	183	Test #3	175		BIG FAIL ←
5	Test #4	243	Test #4	243		Pass
6	Test #5	263	Test #5	260		Fail

IFERROR FUNCTION

IFERROR Syntax:

IFERROR(value, value_if_error)
All **parameters** are required

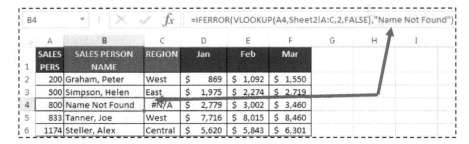

| B4 | ▼ | : | ✕ | ✓ | *fx* | =IFERROR(VLOOKUP(A4,Sheet2!A:C,2,FALSE),"Name Not Found") |

	A	B	C	D	E	F	G	H	I
1	SALES PERS	SALES PERSON NAME	REGION	Jan	Feb	Mar			
2	200	Graham, Peter	West	$ 869	$ 1,092	$ 1,550			
3	500	Simpson, Helen	East	$ 1,975	$ 2,274	$ 2,719			
4	800	Name Not Found	#N/A	$ 2,779	$ 3,002	$ 3,460			
5	833	Tanner, Joe	West	$ 7,716	$ 8,015	$ 8,460			
6	1174	Steller, Alex	Central	$ 5,620	$ 5,843	$ 6,301			

EXAMPLE 3: IFERROR AND THE VLOOKUP

Scenario:

You've been asked to provide a list of first quarter sales by month, for each sales person. However, *if* the Sales Person's name is not available, display the text "**Name Not Found**." To accomplish this, you use a combination of the functions **IFERROR** & **VLOOKUP** to develop the sales report.

WEB ADDRESS & FILE NAME FOR EXERCISE:
https://bentonbooks.wixsite.com/bentonbooks/excel-2019
Example_3_IFERROR.xlsx

Steps To Complete The Exercise:

Sample data:

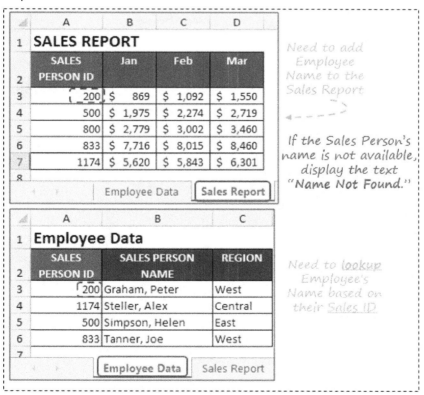

1. Open the Example_3_IFERROR.xlsx spreadsheet

2. Select the tab named **'Sales Report'**

3. Place your cursor in cell **'B3'**

4. From the Ribbon select **Formulas : Lookup & Reference**

5. From the drop-down list, select the option **'VLOOKUP'**

6. In the Function Arguments dialogue box enter the following:

   a. Click cell '**A3**' or enter **A3** in the dialogue box for the **'Lookup_value'**

   b. For **'Table_array'**, click on the tab **'Employee Data'** and select **columns 'A:C'**

   c. Enter the number **2** for '**Col_index_num**'

   d. For '**Range_lookup**' enter **False**

7. Click the '**OK**' button

The following result should now be displayed on the **Sales Report** worksheet:

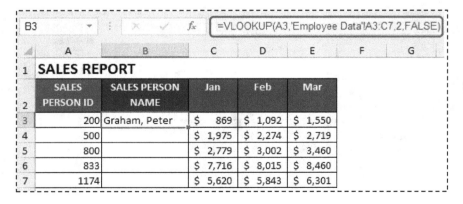

8. Copy and paste the formula down to cells '**B4:B7**'

The following should be the result. *Note: the error **#N/A** in cell '**B5**', this occurs because in the **Table_array (Employee Data)** there is no Sales Person ID for **ID# 800***

	A	B	C	D	E
1	**SALES REPORT**				
2	**SALES PERSON ID**	**SALES PERSON NAME**	**Jan**	**Feb**	**Mar**
3	200	Graham, Peter	$ 869	$ 1,092	$ 1,550
4	500	Simpson, Helen	$ 1,975	$ 2,274	$ 2,719
5	800	#N/A	$ 2,779	$ 3,002	$ 3,460
6	833	Tanner, Joe	$ 7,716	$ 8,015	$ 8,460
7	1174	Steller, Alex	$ 5,620	$ 5,843	$ 6,301

We were asked to provide a list of first quarter sales by month, for each sales person. However, *if* the Sales Person's name is not available, display the text **"Name Not Found."** To address this requirement we will add the function **IFERROR** to our **VLOOKUP** formula.

9. Select cell '**B3**' on the worksheet '**Sales Report**'

10. Add the **IFERROR** formula to the existing **VLOOKUP** function as follows:

```
=IFERROR(VLOOKUP(A3,'Employee Data'!A:C,2,FALSE),"Name Not Found")
```

The following should be the result:

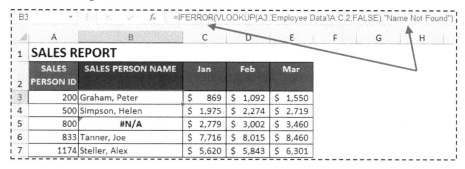

11. Copy and paste this formula down to cells '**B4:B7**'

Note: the previous error of **#N/A** in cell '**B5**' is no longer shown, instead "Name Not Found" is now displayed.

	A	B	C	D	E
1	**SALES REPORT**				
2	**SALES PERSON ID**	**SALES PERSON NAME**	**Jan**	**Feb**	**Mar**
3	200	Graham, Peter	$ 869	$ 1,092	$ 1,550
4	500	Simpson, Helen	$ 1,975	$ 2,274	$ 2,719
5	800	**Name Not Found**	$ 2,779	$ 3,002	$ 3,460
6	833	Tanner, Joe	$ 7,716	$ 8,015	$ 8,460
7	1174	Steller, Alex	$ 5,620	$ 5,843	$ 6,301

You've now created a list of first quarter sales by month, for each sales person and when the Sales Person's name is unavailable, the text **"Name Not Found"** is displayed.

☑ **HELPFUL INFORMATION:**

The *IF*ERROR formula was introduced in Microsoft® Excel® version 2007, prior to this, many of us would use *IS*ERROR. I include an example of *IS*ERROR in this book, because I still see many people use this function in spreadsheets today.

In the exercise above, someone may use the **ISERROR** formula to accomplish the same thing as **IFERROR**, below is an example of the how the formula would be written:

```
=IF(ISERROR(VLOOKUP(A5,'Employee Data'!A:C,2,FALSE)),
"Name Not Found",(VLOOKUP(A5,'Employee Data'!A:C,2,FALSE)))
```

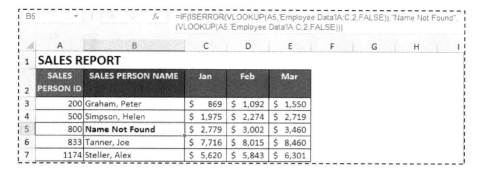

As you can see, **IFERROR** greatly simplifies this type of functionality.

In the workplace we're often given reports or query results in formats incompatible with each other, requiring the data be transformed before further analysis or reporting can be completed.

In this chapter we explore some challenges that may arise when using the VLOOKUP formula such as:

- What to do when you don't have a unique **Lookup_value**
- When the **Lookup_value** is listed more than once in the **Table_array**

WHEN YOU DON'T HAVE A UNIQUE LOOKUP_VALUE

A common issue when using the VLOOKUP formula is you will *not* have a unique **Lookup_value**. In the previous examples, we used a distinct sales person ID number. However, **how would we handle a situation where we only had a list of first and last names?** To tackle this question, we're going to introduce the function called **CONCAT** or CONCATENATE *(Excel® v2013 & earlier)*. Please skip this section if you're already familiar with how concatenation works.

CONCAT FUNCTION

FUNCTION	DEFINITION
CONCAT / CONCATENATE	Joins two or more cells together, also allows the option to insert additional text into the merged cell

Function Syntax:	Function Syntax:	
CONCAT(text)	CONCATENATE(text)	*Excel version*
text is required	text is required	*2013 & earlier*

	A	B	C	D
	SALES PERSON FIRST NAME	SALES PERSON LAST NAME	FORMULA	Merged cells 'B2' & 'A2', Last Name, followed by a comma and space, then First Name
1				
2	Jack	Smith	=CONCATENATE(B2,", ",A2)	Smith, Jack

Alternatively, you may perform the same type of functionality, by using the **ampersand (&) symbol**. This is how many intermediate and advanced Excel® users typically execute this command. Please see below for an example:

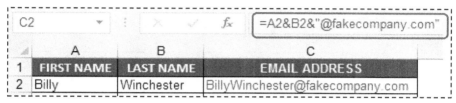

	A	B	C
1	FIRST NAME	LAST NAME	EMAIL ADDRESS
2	Billy	Winchester	BillyWinchester@fakecompany.com

With C2 showing: =A2&B2&"@fakecompany.com"

EXAMPLE 4: COMBINING COLUMNS TO CREATE A UNIQUE LOOKUP_VALUE

Scenario:

You've been given a spreadsheet containing two tabs:

- Tab 1 = A list of employees and their associated metadata
- Tab 2 = Sales Associates first quarter sales

You need to lookup what sales region each employee belongs too. You attempt to use the VLOOKUP formula, however upon further review of the two tabs, you discover the sales report contains only the sales person's first and last name, *but not their sales person ID number*. Therefore, you're not sure what the unique **Lookup_value** should be. *You're unable to lookup based on first or last name alone, because more than one employee has either the same first or last name.* You decide to use the CONCAT function to create a unique **Lookup_value**.

Steps To Complete The Exercise:

Sample data:

Need to add Employee Region to the Sales Report

	A	B	C	D	E
1	SALES PERSON FIRST	SALES PERSON LAST	Jan	Feb	Mar
2	**Peter**	Danner	$ 4,449	$ 7,048	$ 5,746
3	Maggie	**Graham**	$ 3,973	$ 6,251	$ 7,719
4	**Peter**	**Graham**	$ 1,975	$ 2,274	$ 2,719
5	Helen	Simpson	$ 7,716	$ 8,015	$ 8,460
6	Alex	Steller	$ 2,779	$ 3,002	$ 3,460
7	Joe	Tanner	$ 5,620	$ 5,843	$ 6,301
8	Elizabeth	Winchester	$ 869	$ 1,092	$ 1,550
9					

Employee Data | **Sales Report** | ⊕

No Sales Person ID, can't use First or Last Name as the Lookup_value, because more than one employee has either the same first or last name

	A	B	C	D	E
1	SALES PERSON ID	SALES PERSON LAST	SALES PERSON FIRST	SALES REGION	MANAGER ID
2	100	Winchester	Elizabeth	West	50
3	200	Graham	Peter	West	50
4	300	Steller	Alex	Central	30
5	400	Simpson	Helen	East	40
6	500	Tanner	Joe	West	50
7	600	Graham	Maggie	Central	30
8	700	Danner	Peter	East	40
9					

Contains the employee's sales 'Region'

Employee Data | Sales Report | ⊕

1. Open the Example_4_CONCAT.xlsx spreadsheet

2. Select the tab named **'Sales Report'**

3. **Insert** a column on the sales report before '**SALES PERSON FIRST**'
   A. Right-click the current **Column 'A'** *(SALES PERSON FIRST)*

B. From the drop-down box select the option '**Insert**'

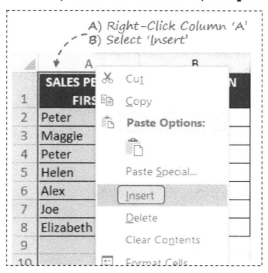

4. Label the new **column 'A'**, cell **'A1'** as **'VLOOKUP ID'** *(this column is going to become our new Lookup_value)*

The sales report should now look similar to the following:

	A	B	C	D	E	F
1	VLOOKUP ID	SALES PERSON FIRST	SALES PERSON LAST	Jan	Feb	Mar
2		Peter	Danner	$ 4,449	$ 7,048	$ 5,746
3		Maggie	Graham	$ 3,973	$ 6,251	$ 7,719
4		Peter	Graham	$ 1,975	$ 2,274	$ 2,719
5		Helen	Simpson	$ 7,716	$ 8,015	$ 8,460
6		Alex	Steller	$ 2,779	$ 3,002	$ 3,460
7		Joe	Tanner	$ 5,620	$ 5,843	$ 6,301
8		Elizabeth	Winchester	$ 869	$ 1,092	$ 1,550

5. Place your cursor in cell **'A2'**

6. From the Ribbon select **Formulas : Text**

7. From the drop-down list, select the option **'CONCAT'**

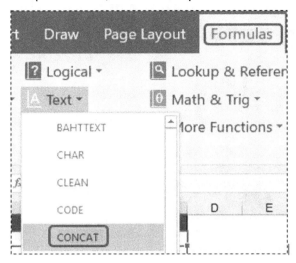

8. In the Function Arguments dialogue box enter the following:
   a. **Text1** box click cell **'C2'** or enter **C2**

   b. **Text2** box enter a hyphen **-** *(dash or minus symbol)*

   c. **Text3** box enter the text **'B2'** or enter **B2**

9. Click the **'OK'** button

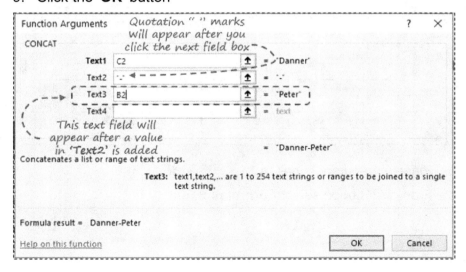

10. Copy and paste the **CONCAT** formula down cells '**A3:A8**'

A2		fx	=CONCAT(C2,"-",B2)			
	A	B	C	D	E	F
1	VLOOKUP ID	SALES PERSON FIRST	SALES PERSON LAST	Jan	Feb	Mar
2	Danner-Peter	Peter	Danner	$ 4,449	$ 7,048	$ 5,746
3		Maggie	Graham	$ 3,973	$ 6,251	$ 7,719
4		Peter	Graham	$ 1,975	$ 2,274	$ 2,719
5		Helen	Simpson	$ 7,716	$ 8,015	$ 8,460
6		Alex	Steller	$ 2,779	$ 3,002	$ 3,460
7		Joe	Tanner	$ 5,620	$ 5,843	$ 6,301
8		Elizabeth	Winchester	$ 869	$ 1,092	$ 1,550

Copy formula to cells 'A3:A8'

11. Copy this formula to cells '**A3:A8**'

12. Press the '**Esc**' *(Escape)* button on your keyboard twice

13. **Insert** a column on the sales report between '**SALES PERSON LAST**' & '**Jan**'
    A. Right-click the current **Column 'D'** *(Jan)*
    B. From the drop-down box select the option '**Insert**'

A) *Right Click column 'D'*
B) *Select 'Insert'*

	A	B	C	D		
1	VLOOKUP ID	SALES PERSON FIRST	SALES PERSON LAST	Jan		Cut
2	Danner-Peter	Peter	Danner	$ 4,4		Copy
3	Graham-Maggie	Maggie	Graham	$ 3,9		Paste Options:
4	Graham-Peter	Peter	Graham	$ 1,9		
5	Simpson-Helen	Helen	Simpson	$ 7,		Paste Special...
6	Steller-Alex	Alex	Steller	$ 2,		Insert
7	Tanner-Joe	Joe	Tanner	$ 5,		Delete
8	Winchester-Elizabeth	Elizabeth	Winchester	$		Clear Contents

14. Label the new **column 'D'**, cell '**D1**' as '**REGION**'

	A	B	C	D	E	F	G
1	VLOOKUP ID	SALES PERSON FIRST	SALES PERSON LAST	REGION	Jan	Feb	Mar
2	Danner-Peter	Peter	Danner		$ 4,449	$ 7,048	$ 5,746
3	Graham-Maggie	Maggie	Graham		$ 3,973	$ 6,251	$ 7,719
4	Graham-Peter	Peter	Graham		$ 1,975	$ 2,274	$ 2,719
5	Simpson-Helen	Helen	Simpson		$ 7,716	$ 8,015	$ 8,460
6	Steller-Alex	Alex	Steller		$ 2,779	$ 3,002	$ 3,460
7	Tanner-Joe	Joe	Tanner		$ 5,620	$ 5,843	$ 6,301
8	Winchester-Elizab	Elizabeth	Winchester		$ 869	$ 1,092	$ 1,550

15. Select the **'Employee Data'** worksheet

	A	B	C	D	E
1	SALES PERSON ID	SALES PERSON LAST	SALES PERSON FIRST	SALES REGION	MANAGER ID
2	100	Winchester	Elizabeth	West	50
3	200	Graham	Peter	West	50
4	300	Steller	Alex	Central	30
5	400	Simpson	Helen	East	40
6	500	Tanner	Joe	West	50
7	600	Graham	Maggie	Central	30
8	700	Danner	Peter	East	40

Employee Data | Sales Report | ⊕

16. Insert a column before **'SALES PERSON ID'**

17. Label the new **column 'A1'** as 'VLOOKUP ID'

18. In cell **'A2'** apply the following CONCAT formula:
   =CONCAT(C2,"-",D2)

A2	▼	⁝	× ✓ fx	=CONCAT(C2,"-",D2)		

	A	B	C	D	E	F
1	VLOOKUP ID	SALES PERSON ID	SALES PERSON LAST	SALES PERSON FIRST	SALES REGION	MANAGER ID
2	Winchester-Elizabeth	100	Winchester	Elizabeth	West	50
3		200	Graham	Peter	West	50
4		300	Steller	Alex	Central	30
5		400	Simpson	Helen	East	40
6		500	Tanner	Joe	West	50
7		600	Graham	Maggie	Central	30
8		700	Danner	Peter	East	40

19. Copy and paste the CONCAT formula to cells **'A3:A8'**

20. Press the **'Esc'** *(Escape)* button on your keyboard twice

21. Return to the **Sales Report** worksheet

22. Select cell **'D2'** and apply the following VLOOKUP formula:

   =VLOOKUP(A2,'Employee Data'!A:F,5,FALSE)

23. Copy and paste the VLOOKUP formula to cells 'D3:D8'

D2				f_x	=VLOOKUP(A2,'Employee Data'!A:F,5,FALSE)		

	A	B	C	D	E	F	G
		SALES PERSON	SALES PERSON		Jan	Feb	Mar
1	VLOOKUP ID	FIRST	LAST	REGION			
2	Danner-Peter	Peter	Danner	East	$ 4,449	$ 7,048	$ 5,746
3	Graham-Maggie	Maggie	Graham	Central	$ 3,973	$ 6,251	$ 7,719
4	Graham-Peter	Peter	Graham	West	$ 1,975	$ 2,274	$ 2,719
5	Simpson-Helen	Helen	Simpson	East	$ 7,716	$ 8,015	$ 8,460
6	Steller-Alex	Alex	Steller	Central	$ 2,779	$ 3,002	$ 3,460
7	Tanner-Joe	Joe	Tanner	West	$ 5,620	$ 5,843	$ 6,301
8	Winchester-Elizab	Elizabeth	Winchester	West	$ 869	$ 1,092	$ 1,550

24. Highlight cells '**D2:D8**' and click the '**Copy**' button or press **CTL+C** from your keyboard

25. From the '**Paste**' drop-down menu select '**Paste Values**' the '**123**' option *(see page 18 for an example)*

26. After you **paste as a value**, you may delete **column 'A'** on the **Sales Report** worksheet

	A	B	C	D	E	F
	SALES PERSON	SALES PERSON	REGION	Jan	Feb	Mar
1	FIRST	LAST				
2	Peter	Danner	East	$ 4,449	$ 7,048	$ 5,746
3	Maggie	Graham	Central	$ 3,973	$ 6,251	$ 7,719
4	Peter	Graham	West	$ 1,975	$ 2,274	$ 2,719
5	Helen	Simpson	East	$ 7,716	$ 8,015	$ 8,460
6	Alex	Steller	Central	$ 2,779	$ 3,002	$ 3,460
7	Joe	Tanner	West	$ 5,620	$ 5,843	$ 6,301
8	Elizabeth	Winchester	West	$ 869	$ 1,092	$ 1,550

You now have a list of employees, their first quarter sales results, and sales region.

WHAT IS INDEX AND MATCH?

In Example 4 we added a column to each worksheet to create our unique **Lookup_value**, while this method is effective and completes the task, there is another way to accomplish this objective.

By using a combination of the functions called **INDEX + MATCH** we can avoid the need to add additional columns. **INDEX + MATCH** are both a part of the **Lookup & Reference** formula collection, they both evaluate a range of cells, and they each return a value. However, unlike other functions in Excel, **INDEX + MATCH** are seldom used by themselves.

Additionally, **INDEX** has two forms *Array* and *Reference*, the distinction between these two forms is rather esoteric. Essentially, the *Array form* returns a value based on *a specific* cell or cells and the *Reference form* returns a value based on *an intersection* or proximity of a specific row and column. To complicate things further, for Excel® to recognize you're using a dynamic INDEX Array you must type **CTRL+SHIFT+ENTER** *(non-Office 365 platforms)* in order for the function to work properly.

Using **INDEX + MATCH** does indeed take some practice and some Excel® users argue the method described below is more difficult to enter and troubleshoot, not saving the time you'd expect by entering a single formula.

Yet, there are some real advantages to using this approach, such as being able to add and delete columns without breaking your lookup and the ability to lookup information from Left-To-Right versus the VLOOKUP limitation of only Right-To-Left lookups.

For our next exercise we will be using a combination of the functions **INDEX**, **MATCH**, and **CONCAT** however, we _will not_ be using VLOOKUP.

Let's take a quick look at how these functions work.

FUNCTION	DEFINITION
INDEX	The INDEX function *returns a **value*** or the reference to a value in a cell range. INDEX has two forms, Array & Reference. For the purposes of this book, we will be using the *Array form* which returns the value of a specific cell or cells.
MATCH	MATCH searches for a specific value from a cell range and *returns the **position*** of that element.

INDEX FUNCTION (ARRAY FORM)

INDEX Syntax:

`INDEX(array,row_num, [column_num]`

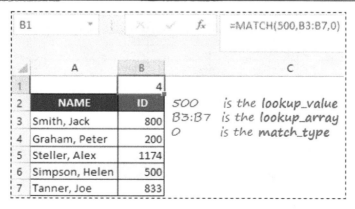

MATCH FUNCTION

MATCH Syntax:

`MATCH(lookup_value,lookup_array, [match_type]`

	A	B	C
1		4	
2	**NAME**	**ID**	500 is the *lookup_value*
3	Smith, Jack	800	B3:B7 is the *lookup_array*
4	Graham, Peter	200	0 is the *match_type*
5	Steller, Alex	1174	
6	Simpson, Helen	500	
7	Tanner, Joe	833	

B1   *fx*   =MATCH(500,B3:B7,0)

EXAMPLE 5: INDEX & MATCH

WEB ADDRESS & FILE NAME FOR EXERCISE:
https://bentonbooks.wixsite.com/bentonbooks/excel-2019
Example_5_INDEX_and_MATCH.xlsx

Steps To Complete The Exercise:

Sample data:

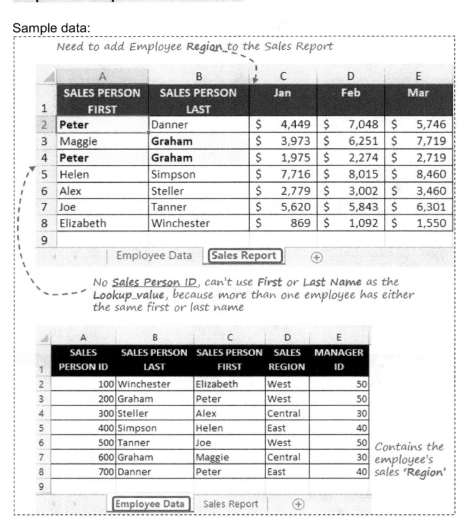

1. Open the Example_5_INDEX_and_MATCH.xlsx spreadsheet
2. Select the tab named **'Sales Report'**
3. Place your cursor in cell **'C2'**

4. From the Ribbon select **Formulas : Lookup & Reference**

5. From the drop-down list, select the option **'MATCH'**

6. In the Function Arguments dialogue box enter the following:
   a. **Lookup_value** box and enter **B2&A2**
   b. **Lookup_array** box click the **'Employee Data' tab and:**
      - Click **column 'B'**
      - Enter the **ampersand (&)** symbol
      - Click **column 'C'**

      Value should be the following:
      ```
      'Employee Data'!B:B&'Employee Data'!C:C
      ```
   c. **Match_Type** enter **0** (zero)

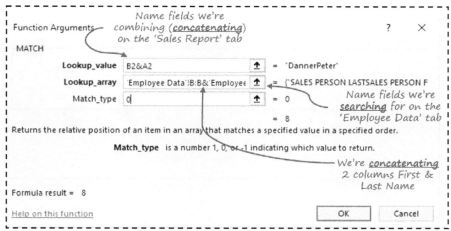

7. Click the '**OK**' button, you will receive the **#VALUE!** error

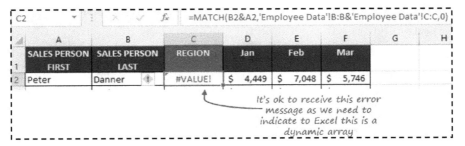

8. Click inside the formula bar for cell '**C2**' *(cursor should be flashing)*

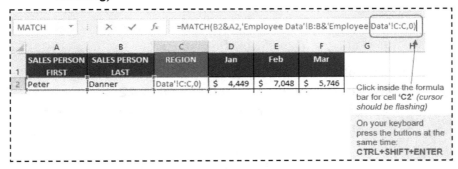

9. On your keyboard, at the same time press the buttons: **CTRL+SHIFT+ENTER**

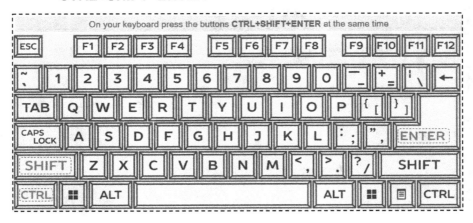

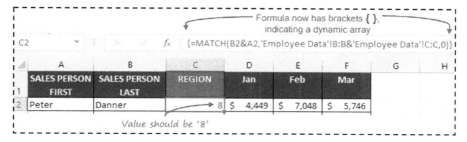

Next, we'll add the **INDEX** function, which will indicate the *REGION* data we want returned.

10. Place your cursor in cell **'C2'** between the = (symbol) and the word **MATCH**

11. Type the following:
    =**INDEX('Employee Data'!D:D,**MATCH(B2&A2,'Employee Data'!B:B&'Employee Data'!C:C,0))

    =INDEX('Employee Data'!D:D,MATCH(B2&A2,'Employee Data'!B:B&'Employee Data'!C:C,0))

12. Press **ENTER** on your keyboard

13. Click inside the formula bar for cell **'C2'** *(cursor should be flashing)*

14. On your keyboard, at the same time press the buttons: **CTRL+SHIFT+ENTER**

15. Copy and paste the formula to cells **'C3:C8'**

	A	B	C	D	E	F
1	SALES PERSON FIRST	SALES PERSON LAST	REGION	Jan	Feb	Mar
2	Peter	Danner	East	$ 4,449	$ 7,048	$ 5,746
3	Maggie	Graham	Central	$ 3,973	$ 6,251	$ 7,719
4	Peter	Graham	West	$ 1,975	$ 2,274	$ 2,719
5	Helen	Simpson	East	$ 7,716	$ 8,015	$ 8,460
6	Alex	Steller	Central	$ 2,779	$ 3,002	$ 3,460
7	Joe	Tanner	West	$ 5,620	$ 5,843	$ 6,301
8	Elizabeth	Winchester	West	$ 869	$ 1,092	$ 1,550

Don't worry if you had trouble with this example, **INDEX + MATCH** are not intuitive functions to learn and do require practice and patience to become proficient with them.

Included with this exercise is a **'Completed Formula'** worksheet if needed.

☑ <u>**HELPFUL INFORMATION:**</u>

While the **CONCAT** and **INDEX + MATCH** functions are helpful when you do not have a unique **Lookup_value,** there are **risks** with these alternatives. In the examples above, if our dataset was larger, there would an increased probability of more than one person having the same first and last name combination. However, sometimes this can't be avoided, the risks are outweighed by the value the VLOOKUP *or* INDEX + MATCH functions bring to task efficiency.

The next section discusses the implications of what happens when you have the same **Lookup_value** listed more than once.

WHEN THE **LOOKUP_VALUE** IS LISTED MORE THAN ONCE IN THE **TABLE_ARRAY**

When the Lookup_value is listed more than once in the Table_array, the VLOOKUP function will always return the ***the first*** **matching Lookup_value it finds in the Table_array**.

Let's walk through an example, using similar sample data as the above for sales and employee, we'll again lookup the employee's sales region:

Sample data (the below Sales Report contains <u>two entries </u>for the same Sales Person ID):

SALES REPORT:

	A	B	C	D	E
1	SALES PERSON ID	SALES PERSON FIRST	SALES PERSON LAST	REGION	Jan
2	700	Peter	Danner		$ 4,449
3	600	Maggie	Graham		$ 3,973
4	200	Peter	Graham		$ 1,975
5	400	Helen	Simpson		$ 7,716
6	300	Alex	Steller		$ 2,779
7	500	Joe	Tanner		$ 5,620
8	100	Elizabeth	Winchester		$ 869
9	300	Butler	Catherine		$ 1,588

EMPLOYEE DATA:

	A	B	C	D	E
1	SALES PERSON ID	SALES PERSON LAST	SALES PERSON FIRST	SALES REGION	MANAGER ID
2	100	Winchester	Elizabeth	West	50
3	200	Graham	Peter	West	50
4	300	Steller	Alex	Central	30
5	400	Simpson	Helen	East	40
6	500	Tanner	Joe	West	50
7	600	Graham	Maggie	Central	30
8	700	Danner	Peter	East	40
9	300	Butler	Catherine	East	40

As the screenshot below shows, the VLOOKUP returned the value for the *first* matching **Lookup_value** it found in the **Table_array**, which in this example, is the region 'Central'.

SALES REPORT:

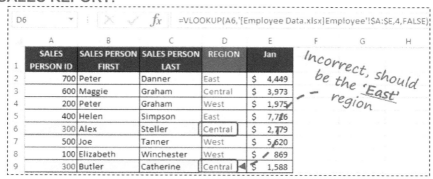

| D6 | f_x | =VLOOKUP(A6,'[Employee Data.xlsx]Employee'!$A:$E,4,FALSE) |

	A	B	C	D	E	F	G	H
1	SALES PERSON ID	SALES PERSON FIRST	SALES PERSON LAST	REGION	Jan			
2	700	Peter	Danner	East	$ 4,449			
3	600	Maggie	Graham	Central	$ 3,973			
4	200	Peter	Graham	West	$ 1,975			
5	400	Helen	Simpson	East	$ 7,716			
6	300	Alex	Steller	Central	$ 2,779			
7	500	Joe	Tanner	West	$ 5,620			
8	100	Elizabeth	Winchester	West	$ 869			
9	300	Butler	Catherine	Central	$ 1,588			

Incorrect, should be the 'East' region

Hopefully, there are system controls in place to prevent a sales person ID from being added more than once. However, I've seen situations where this can happen, especially when migrating data from another system or importing employee information due to an acquisition.

☑ **HELPFUL INFORMATION:**

To address this you could apply the **CONCAT** *or* **INDEX + MATCH** functions to the *sales person's ID*, *first*, and *last name* and make that the unique **Lookup_value**. However, if you're in a position to do so, the best practice would be to change the employee's sales person ID.

An easy way to identify duplicate values is to use **CONDITIONAL FORMATTING**. For example, using the employee sample data:

1. Select **column 'A'**
2. From the Ribbon select **Home**: **Conditional Formatting**
3. From the drop-down box, select the **option 'Highlight Cells Rules'** then **'Duplicate Values…'**

EMPLOYEE DATA:

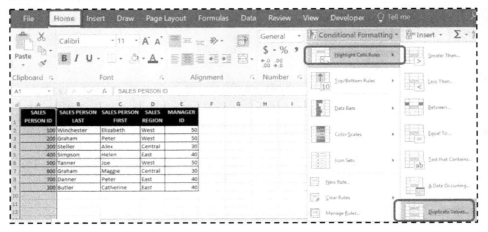

The following dialogue box should appear:

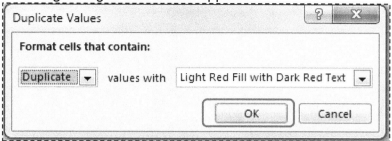

4. Click the '**OK**' button

The following rows should now be highlighted:

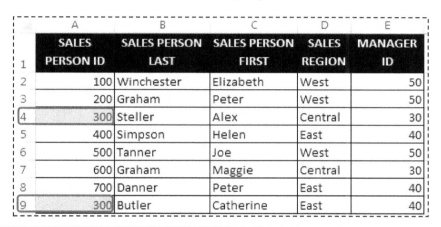

	A	B	C	D	E
1	SALES PERSON ID	SALES PERSON LAST	SALES PERSON FIRST	SALES REGION	MANAGER ID
2	100	Winchester	Elizabeth	West	50
3	200	Graham	Peter	West	50
4	300	Steller	Alex	Central	30
5	400	Simpson	Helen	East	40
6	500	Tanner	Joe	West	50
7	600	Graham	Maggie	Central	30
8	700	Danner	Peter	East	40
9	300	Butler	Catherine	East	40

To remove the Conditional Formatting:

1. From the Ribbon select **Home : Conditional Formatting**

2. Select '**C**lear Rules' and either option:
   a. Clear Rules from **S**elect Cells
   b. Clear Rules from **E**ntire Sheet

In this chapter we continue to build on the lessons from chapters 3 & 4 by combining functions to extend our VLOOKUP capabilities, the following two exercises are reviewed:

1. How to use the VLOOKUP to categorize data
2. Using the VLOOKUP to calculate a number based on specific criteria

EXAMPLE 6: HOW TO USE THE VLOOKUP TO CATEGORIZE DATA

Scenario:

You've been asked to categorize customers by the number of purchases they've made into four tier levels:

```
1) Purchases of  25 – 50 = Bronze
2) Purchases of  51 – 75 = Silver
3) Purchases of  76 – 99 = Gold
4) Purchases of 100+     = Platinum
```

- If they've made less than 25 purchases, display the text *'No Tier'*

To accomplish this, you will use a combination of the functions **IFERROR** & **VLOOKUP** to develop the sales report.

WEB ADDRESS & FILE NAME FOR EXERCISE:
https://bentonbooks.wixsite.com/bentonbooks/excel-2019
Example_6_Categorization.xlsx

Steps To Complete The Exercise:

Sample data:

	A	B	C
1	**CUSTOMER NAME**	**PURCHASES**	**TIER**
2	Alexander, Nora	75	
3	Barnes, Mia	26	
4	Bennett, Lucy	82	
5	Bryant, Julia	75	
6	Butler, Jane	11	
7	Coleman, Ivy	51	
8	Diaz, Isabella	108	
9	Flores, Iris	71	
10	Foster, Hazel	51	
11	Gonzales, Julia	35	
12	Griffin, Evelyn	90	
13	Hayes, Emilia	67	

1. Open the Example_6_Categorization.xlsx spreadsheet

Before entering our **IFERROR + VLOOKUP** function we must prepare our spreadsheet with the requested customer tier levels, this will be our table_array.

2. In cell '**E1**' or enter '**PURCHASE COUNT**'

3. In cell '**F1**' or enter '**TIER LEVELS**'

4. In cells '**E2:E5**' enter the following:
   - Cell '**E2**' = 25
   - Cell '**E3**' = 51
   - Cell '**E4**' = 76
   - Cell '**E5**' = 100

5. In cells '**F2:F5**' enter the following:
   - Cell '**F2**' = Bronze
   - Cell '**F3**' = Silver
   - Cell '**F4**' = Gold
   - Cell '**F5**' = Platinum

When creating our categories to be searched (table_array), the data must be sorted in *Ascending* or *Descending* order. Also, since the purchase count is a range, the lookup_value must be entered by the minimum number eligible for each tier level, for example 25 for the range between 25 - 50.

	A	B	C	D	E	F
1	CUSTOMER NAME	PURCHASES	TIER		PURCHASE COUNT	TIER LEVELS
2	Alexander, Nora	75			25	Bronze
3	Barnes, Mia	26			51	Silver
4	Bennett, Lucy	82			76	Gold
5	Bryant, Julia	75			100	Platinum

The categories to be searched (table_array), the data must be sorted in Ascending or Descending order.

The lookup_value must be entered by the minimum number eligible for each tier level, for example 25 for the range between 25 - 50

6. Place your cursor in cell **'C2'**

7. From the Ribbon select **Formulas : Lookup & Reference**

8. From the drop-down list, select the option **'VLOOKUP'**

9. In the Function Arguments dialogue box enter the following:

   A. Click cell 'B2' or enter **B2** in the dialogue box for the **'Lookup_value'**

   B. For **'Table_array'**, select **cells 'E2:F5'**

   C. Enter the number **2** for **'Col_index_num'**

   D. For '**Range_lookup'** enter **True** *(to return an approximate match)*

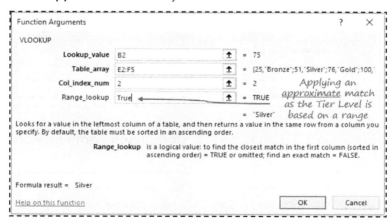

10. Click the **'OK'** button

The following should be the result:

C2				f_x	=VLOOKUP(B2,E2:F5,2,TRUE)

	A	B	C	D	E	F
1	CUSTOMER NAME	PURCHASES	TIER		PURCHASE COUNT	TIER LEVELS
2	Alexander, Nora	75	Silver		25	Bronze
3	Barnes, Mia	26			51	Silver
4	Bennett, Lucy	82			76	Gold
5	Bryant, Julia	75			100	Platinum

11. Select cell **'C2'**

12. Add the U.S. dollar symbol **$** to the 'Table_array'. This will prevent our cell range (Table_array) from changing:

    =VLOOKUP(B2,$E$2:$F$5,2,TRUE)

13. Add the IFERROR formula to the existing VLOOKUP function as follows:

    =**IFERROR(**VLOOKUP(B2,E2:F5,2,TRUE)**,"No Tier")**

14. Copy and paste this formula down to cells **'C3:C31'**

The following should be the result:

C2				f_x	=IFERROR(VLOOKUP(B2,$E$2:$F$5,2,TRUE),"No Tier")

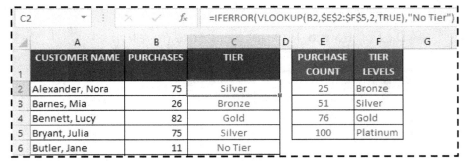

	A	B	C	D	E	F	G
1	CUSTOMER NAME	PURCHASES	TIER		PURCHASE COUNT	TIER LEVELS	
2	Alexander, Nora	75	Silver		25	Bronze	
3	Barnes, Mia	26	Bronze		51	Silver	
4	Bennett, Lucy	82	Gold		76	Gold	
5	Bryant, Julia	75	Silver		100	Platinum	
6	Butler, Jane	11	No Tier				

Included with this exercise is a **'Completed Formula'** worksheet if needed.

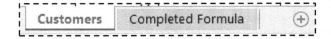

EXAMPLE 7: USING THE VLOOKUP TO CALCULATE BONUSES

Scenario:

You've been asked to determine the following for each Sales Person:

A. If they are eligible for a bonus, based on their sales being greater than or equal to $5,000

B. If yes, what is their bonus rate?

C. Based on their eligible bonus rate, calculate the dollar amount owed to them

D. If they do not qualify for a bonus, display the text **'Not Eligible'**

To accomplish this, you will use a combination of the functions **IF** & **VLOOKUP** to develop the sales report.

WEB ADDRESS & FILE NAME FOR EXERCISE:

https://bentonbooks.wixsite.com/bentonbooks/excel-2019
Example_7_Bonus_Calculation.xlsx

Steps To Complete The Exercise:

Sample data:

Workbook contains **2 worksheets**

	A SALES PERSON	B SALES	C BONUS AMOUNT?
1			
2	Steller, Alex	$ 6,134	
3	Graham, Maggie	$ 4,148	
4	Dockery, Kevin	$ 9,373	
5	Simpson, Helen	$ 2,309	
6	Danner, Peter	$ 2,844	
7	Butler, Catherine	$ 3,921	
8	Winchester, Elizabeth	$ 2,448	
9	Graham, Peter	$ 8,708	
10	Tanner, Joe	$ 7,995	
11	Arnold, Mike	$ 11,052	

1 Sales Report | Bonus Rate ⊕

	A FROM	B TO	C RATE
1			
2	$5,000	$6,999	2%
3	$7,000	$7,999	3%
4	$8,000	$8,999	4%
5	$9,000	$9,999	5%
6			

2 Sales | Bonus Rate

49

PART 1 the IF function:

1. Open the Example_7_Bonus_Calculation.xlsx spreadsheet

2. Select the tab named **'Sales Report'** and place your cursor in cell **'C2'**

3. From the Ribbon select **Formulas : Logical**, from the drop-down list, select the option **'IF'**

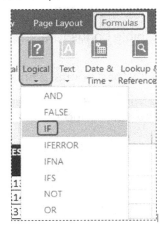

4. In the Function Arguments dialogue box enter the following:

   a. Enter **B2>=5000** in the dialogue box for the **'Logic_test'** *(this is the dollar amount to evaluate if the Sales Person is eligible for a bonus)*

   b. For **'Value_if_true'**, enter **"Y"** *(this is a temporary value, to verify the first part of the formula is working, this will eventually be replaced with the Vlookup function)*

   c. For **'Value_if_false'**, enter **"Not Eligible"** *(text to display if the Sales Person sales were $4,999 or less)*

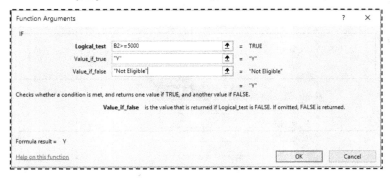

5. Click the '**OK**' button

6. Copy and paste this formula to cells '**C3:C11**'

The following should now be displayed. We've verified the first stage of the formula is working correctly and we know there are five sales people eligible for a bonus, next we'll calculate the amount.

C2				f_x	=IF(B2>=5000,"Y","Not Eligible")		
	A		B		C	D	E
1	SALES PERSON		SALES		BONUS AMOUNT?		
2	Steller, Alex		$ 6,134		Y		
3	Graham, Maggie		$ 4,148		Not Eligible		
4	Dockery, Kevin		$ 9,373		Y		
5	Simpson, Helen		$ 2,309		Not Eligible		
6	Danner, Peter		$ 2,844		Not Eligible		
7	Butler, Catherine		$ 3,921		Not Eligible		
8	Winchester, Elizabeth		$ 2,448		Not Eligible		
9	Graham, Peter		$ 8,708		Y		
10	Tanner, Joe		$ 7,995		Y		
11	Arnold, Mike		$ 11,052		Y		

PART 2 the VLOOKUP function:

7. Select cell '**C2**'

8. Highlight the Value_if_true **"Y"**

9. From the Ribbon select **Formulas : Lookup & Reference**

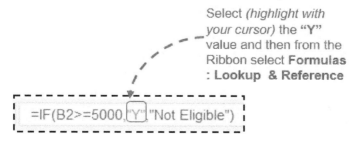

Select *(highlight with your cursor)* the **"Y"** value and then from the Ribbon select **Formulas : Lookup & Reference**

=IF(B2>=5000,"Y","Not Eligible")

10. From the drop-down list, select the option '**VLOOKUP**'

11. In the Function Arguments dialogue box enter the following:

   a. Click cell '**B2**' or enter **B2** in the dialogue box for the '**Lookup_value**' *(the sales number to evaluate)*

   b. For '**Table_array**', click on the tab '**Bonus Rate**' and select columns '**A:C**' *(this is the range of cells we're searching)*

   c. Enter the number **3** for '**Col_index_num**' *(this column contains the bonus rate)*

   d. For '**Range_lookup**' enter **True** *(to return an approximate match)*

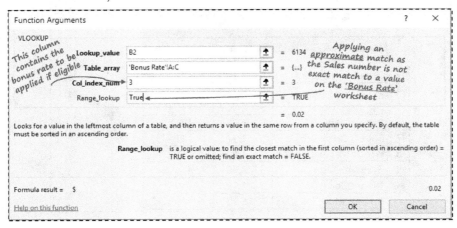

12. Click the '**OK**' button

The following should now be displayed, we've verified 2% is the correct multiplier for the bonus rate for sales greater than $5,000, but less than $7,000:

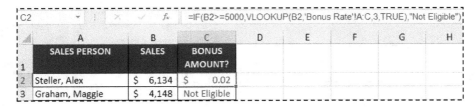

```
=IF(B2>=5000,VLOOKUP(B2,'Bonus Rate'!A:C,3,TRUE),"Not Eligible")
```

PART 3 of the formula:

13. To calculate the dollar amount owed to the sales person if eligible, place your cursor in cell '**C2**'

14. Modify the formula as follows:

```
=IF(B2>=5000,(VLOOKUP(B2,'Bonus Rate'!A:C,3,TRUE)*B2),"Not Eligible")
```

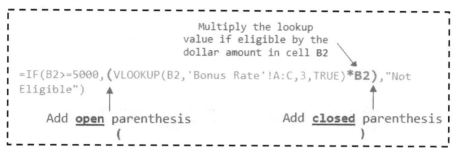

15. Copy this formula to cells '**C3:C11**'

The following should now be displayed, we've completed the sales report per the requirements requested:

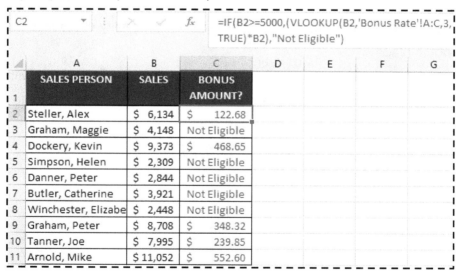

C2				f_x	=IF(B2>=5000,(VLOOKUP(B2,'Bonus Rate'!A:C,3, TRUE)*B2),"Not Eligible")			

	A	B	C	D	E	F	G
1	SALES PERSON	SALES	BONUS AMOUNT?				
2	Steller, Alex	$ 6,134	$ 122.68				
3	Graham, Maggie	$ 4,148	Not Eligible				
4	Dockery, Kevin	$ 9,373	$ 468.65				
5	Simpson, Helen	$ 2,309	Not Eligible				
6	Danner, Peter	$ 2,844	Not Eligible				
7	Butler, Catherine	$ 3,921	Not Eligible				
8	Winchester, Elizabe	$ 2,448	Not Eligible				
9	Graham, Peter	$ 8,708	$ 348.32				
10	Tanner, Joe	$ 7,995	$ 239.85				
11	Arnold, Mike	$ 11,052	$ 552.60				

Included with this exercise is a '**Completed Formula**' worksheet if needed.

A common real-world challenge when looking-up data is similar but not exact matches. For example, your organization has separate *Sales* and *Finance* systems and each capture **'Company Name'** a different way.

ACCOUNTS RECEIVABLE system	SALES system
ABC Stores Inc.	ABC Stores
DD Consulting Partners	DD Consulting

Same company, but the name is slightly different depending on which system is being utilized. This frequently happens when applications are integrated or when data entry / quality standards are not in place.

Another instance is when a suffix or prefix is associated with either the lookup or table_array value. Some common examples include:

PREFIX	SUFFIX
Dr	Assc
Hon	Corp
Mr.	Inc
Mrs.	Ltd
Ms.	LLC

- **Mrs.** Joan Teller
- Benton Books **LLC**

The **VLOOKUP** in combination with the **CONCAT** and **Wildcard** functionality provides a viable alternative to analysis when an exact match (lookup_value) is not available.

WILDCARD FUNCTIONALITY

Wildcard functionality in Excel® uses 1 of three special charters in place of *or* in combination with additional functions to assist in searching for *similar*, but not exact content. These three special charters are:

- * (asterisk)
- ? (question mark)
- ~ (tilde)

In the case of the VLOOKUP the most often used is the * **(asterisk).** The * **(asterisk)** wildcard character indicates to Excel® to search *for any matching values* in the table_array, contained in the lookup_value. The asterisk * inside double quotation marks " " signifies a *variable value* and for Excel® to *essentially ignore* this variable value when searching.

Let's say you wanted to lookup Sales System information, but could not match exactly on company name. The syntax would *conceptually* look like the following:

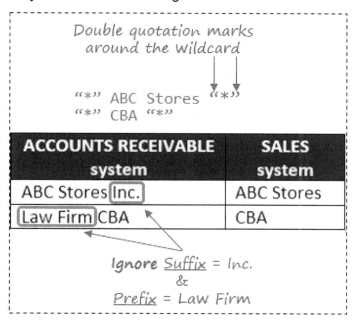

Below is a formula example:

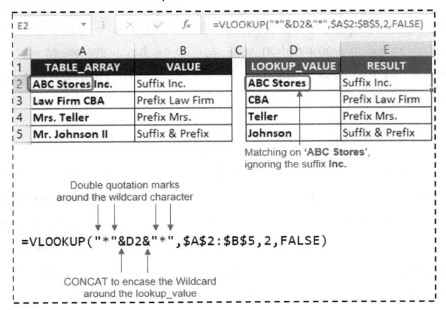

However, there are limitations with the **Wildcard** functionality such as:

- The lookup_value can not contain any values *not in* the table_array. For example, if your lookup_value is 'ABC Stores *Inc.*', but the table_array contains only 'ABC Stores', you'll receive the #N/A error.

- Even with Wildcard functionality the VLOOKUP function will always return the value for ***the first*** **matching Lookup_value it finds in the Table_array**.

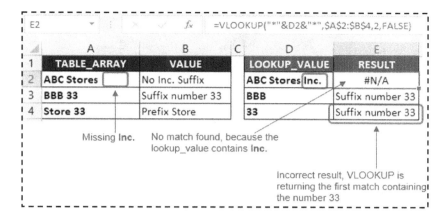

EXAMPLE 8: THE WILDCARD VLOOKUP

Scenario:

You've been asked to provide a report by Sales Rep, each company they represent, and their first quarter sales.

- The **Sales** database, contains the Q1 sales and displays the full company name *including their suffixes*.

- The **Account Management** system includes the Sales Rep and each company they represent. However, the company name *may* or *may not* include suffixes.

To accomplish this, you will use the **VLOOKUP** in combination with **CONCAT** and **Wildcard** functionality to complete the request.

WEB ADDRESS & FILE NAME FOR EXERCISE:
https://bentonbooks.wixsite.com/bentonbooks/excel-2019
Example_8_Wildcard.xlsx

Steps To Complete The Exercise:

Sample data:

	A	B	C	D	E
1	COMPANY NAME	Jan	Feb	Mar	Q1_TOTAL
2	AAA LLC	$1,709	$4,641	$4,174	$10,524
3	ABC Stores Worldwide	$4,491	$4,212	$2,371	$11,074
4	CCC Enterprises	$4,263	$3,287	$1,252	$8,802
5	DD Consulting Co	$3,962	$1,793	$2,806	$8,561
6	E-Inc.	$3,968	$3,359	$1,681	$9,008
7	MMM Technologies	$3,372	$1,776	$4,640	$9,788
8	GGG Inc.	$1,803	$3,449	$3,050	$8,302
9	RRR Ltd.	$3,990	$3,447	$1,828	$9,265
10	SSS Assc.	$3,394	$1,864	$4,787	$10,045
11	TTT Worldwide	$1,144	$2,711	$1,708	$5,563
12	UUU LLC		$3,112	$1,778	$2,110	$7,000
13	VVV LLP	$1,574	$2,046	$4,449	$8,069
14	WWW Logistics	$3,213	$1,659	$1,965	$6,837
15	YYY Corp	$1,272	$4,998	$4,623	$10,893
16	ZZZ Properties	$2,835	$2,695	$2,196	$7,726

Sales System

	A	B	C
1	COMPANY	SALES REP	Q1
2	RRR	Gonzales, Julia	
3	SSS	Gonzales, Julia	
4	AAA	Graham, Maggie	
5	GGG	Graham, Maggie	
6	ZZZ	Graham, Maggie	
7	ABC Stores	Graham, Peter	
8	TTT	Graham, Peter	
9	CCC	Simpson, Helen	
10	UUU	Simpson, Helen	
11	DD Consulting	Steller, Alex	
12	VVV	Steller, Alex	
13	E-Inc	Tanner, Joe	
14	WWW	Tanner, Joe	
15	MMM	Winchester, Elizabeth	
16	YYY	Winchester, Elizabeth	

Account Management System

Need to lookup company name without suffixes (such as: LLC, Inc. Co) and return the Q1 values

1. Open the Example_8_Wildcard.xlsx spreadsheet
2. Select the tab named **'Sales Rep List'**

3. Place your cursor is cell **'C2'**
4. From the Ribbon select **Formulas : Lookup & Reference**

5. From the drop-down list, select the option **'VLOOKUP'**

6. In the Function Arguments dialogue box enter the following:

   A. For the **'Lookup_value'** enter the following:

   ### "*"&A2&"*"

   B. For **'Table_array'**, click the tab **'Company Sales'** and select **columns 'A:E'**

   C. Enter the number **5** for **'Col_index_num'**

   D. For **'Range_lookup'** enter **False**

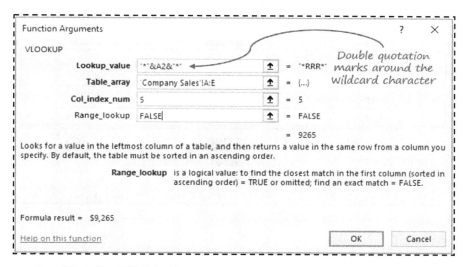

7. Click the **'OK'** button

8. Copy and paste the formula to cells **'C3:C16'**

The following should be the result:

	A	B	C
1	COMPANY	SALES REP	Q1
2	RRR	Gonzales, Julia	$9,265
3	SSS	Gonzales, Julia	$10,045
4	AAA	Graham, Maggie	$10,524
5	GGG	Graham, Maggie	$8,302
6	ZZZ	Graham, Maggie	$7,726
7	ABC Stores	Graham, Peter	$11,074
8	TTT	Graham, Peter	$5,563
9	CCC	Simpson, Helen	$8,802
10	UUU	Simpson, Helen	$7,000
11	DD Consulting	Steller, Alex	$8,561
12	VVV	Steller, Alex	$8,069
13	E-Inc	Tanner, Joe	$9,008
14	WWW	Tanner, Joe	$6,837
15	MMM	Winchester, Elizabeth	$9,788
16	YYY	Winchester, Elizabeth	$10,893

Included with this exercise is a **'Completed Formula'** worksheet if needed.

Company Sales	Sales Rep List	Completed Formula	⊕

For our last example, we'll review applying the VLOOKUP across multiple worksheets and workbooks. The VLOOKUP can be very useful when consolidating data from multiple spreadsheets. It is most beneficial when the spreadsheets being consolidated are formatted and structured <u>in the same way</u>.

This exercise will require building a **nested VLOOKUP** with the **IFERROR** function, once completed this formula is going be very long. However, by building the <u>**function in stages**</u>, we will minimize errors. Also, if we run into problems it will be easier to troubleshoot, because we know the previous parts of the formula are working.

EXAMPLE 9: APPLYING A VLOOKUP ACROSS MULTIPLE WORKSHEETS & WORKBOOKS

Scenario:

A new sales management position has been created to oversee three sales regions. This new manager has been given a list of employee IDs, but does not know each employee's name and sales region. She has asked you to pull together all the employee data and create a *consolidated* **Manager's report**.

WEB ADDRESS & FILE NAMES FOR EXERCISE:
https://bentonbooks.wixsite.com/bentonbooks/excel-2019
Example_9_ManagersReport.xlsx
Example_9_EmployeeData.xlsx

Steps To Complete The Exercise:

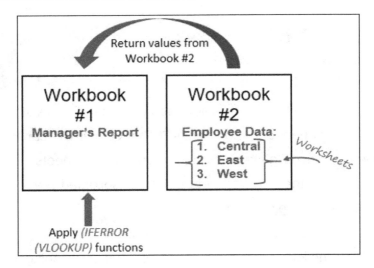

Sample data:

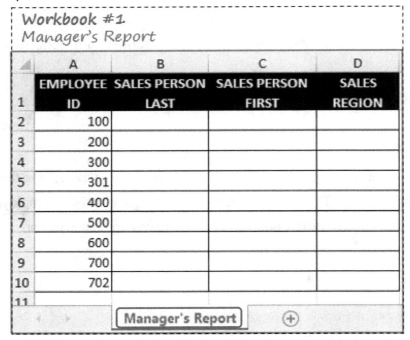

Workbook #2

Employee Data, contains **3 worksheets**

	A	B	C	D
1	EMPLOYEE ID	SALES PERSON LAST	SALES PERSON FIRST	SALES REGION
2	300	Steller	Alex	Central
3	600	Graham	Maggie	Central
4	702	Dockery	Kevin	Central
5				

1

Central | East | West | ⊕

	A	B	C	D
1	EMPLOYEE ID	SALES PERSON LAST	SALES PERSON FIRST	SALES REGION
2	400	Simpson	Helen	East
3	700	Danner	Peter	East
4	301	Butler	Catherine	East
5				

2

Central | East | West | ⊕

	A	B	C	D
1	EMPLOYEE ID	SALES PERSON LAST	SALES PERSON FIRST	SALES REGION
2	100	Winchester	Elizabeth	West
3	200	Graham	Peter	West
4	500	Tanner	Joe	West
5				

3

Central | East | West | ⊕

1. Open the Example_9_EmployeeData.xlsx spreadsheet
2. Open the Example_9_ManagersReport.xlsx spreadsheet

3. On the Example_9_**ManagersReport**.xlsx select cell **'B2'**

4. From the Ribbon select **Formulas : Lookup & Reference**

5. From the drop-down list, select the option **'VLOOKUP'**

6. In the Function Arguments dialogue box enter the following:
   a. Click cell **'A2'** or enter **A2** in the dialogue box for the **'Lookup_value'**

   b. For **'Table_array'**, click the workbook Example_9_**EmployeeData**.xlsx, the 'Central' worksheet and select columns **'A:D'**

   c. Enter the number **2** for '**Col_index_num**'

   d. For '**Range_lookup**' enter **False**

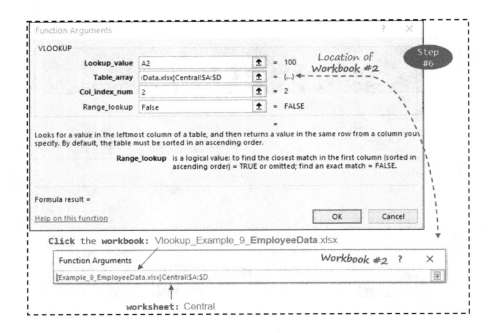

7. Click the '**OK**' button

You'll receive the **#N/A** message, this is <u>OK</u> and to be expected. We'll address this as we go.

Workbook #1 (Manager's Report)

| B2 | ▼ | : | × | ✓ | fx | =VLOOKUP(A2,[Example_9_EmployeeData.xlsx]Central!$A:$D,2,FALSE) |

	A	B	C	D	E	F	G	H
1	EMPLOYEE ID	SALES PERSON LAST	SALES PERSON FIRST	SALES REGION				
2	①)0	#N/A	◄- - -.					
3	200							
4	300							
5	301							
6	400							
7	500							
8	600							
9	700							
10	702							

It is 'OK' we received the #N/A error, we'll address as we build the formula

Manager's Report   ⊕

8. Copy and paste the VLOOKUP formula down to cells **'B3: B10'**, *only Rows 4, 8, & 10* should now have values:

	A	B	C	D
1	EMPLOYEE ID	SALES PERSON LAST	SALES PERSON FIRST	SALES REGION
2	100	#N/A		
3	200	#N/A		
4	300	Steller		
5	301	#N/A		
6	400	#N/A		
7	500	#N/A		
8	600	Graham		
9	700	#N/A		
10	702	Dockery		
11				
12				

Manager's Report   ⊕

9. Next, add the **IFERROR** function to the **VLOOKUP** formula, return to cell **'B2'** and enter the following:

```
=IFERROR(VLOOKUP(A2,[Example_9_EmployeeData.xlsx]
    Central!$A:$D,2,FALSE),"Name Not Found")
```

10. Copy the updated IFERROR & VLOOKUP formula to cells **'B3:B10'**

Workbook #1 (Manager's Report)

B2				f_x	=IFERROR(VLOOKUP(A2,[Example_9_EmployeeData.xlsx]Central!$A:$D,2, FALSE),"Name Not Found")				

	A	B	C	D	E	F	G	H	I
1	EMPLOYEE ID	SALES PERSON LAST	SALES PERSON FIRST	SALES REGION					
2	100	Name Not Found							
3	200	Name Not Found							
4	300	Steller							
5	301	Name Not Found							
6	400	Name Not Found							
7	500	Name Not Found							
8	600	Graham							
9	700	Name Not Found							
10	702	Dockery							

Manager's Report ⊕

We've completed the first part of our nested VLOOKUP function. Next, we'll add the second element to our formula for the worksheet **'East'** region.

Remember, <u>we're building our formula in stages</u>, verifying each segment works before moving on to the next step.

Unfortunately, there is no wizard for building nested functions, therefore we'll need to augment this formula manually. In this example, *we know the remaining region worksheets are structured in the same layout as the 'Central' region*, therefore we can copy a portion of our existing formula and modify it for regions **'East'** and **'West'**.

11. Return to the Example_9_**ManagersReport**.xlsx spreadsheet and select cell **'B2'**

12. Select *(highlight)* and copy (CTRL+C) this section of the formula:
    `=IFERROR(VLOOKUP(A2,[Example_9_EmployeeData.xlsx]Central!` `$A:$D,2,FALSE),"Name Not Found")`

13. **Paste (CTRL+V)** <u>*before*</u> `"Name Not Found")`

14. Change the text from `Central!` to `East!`

15. Add the additional parenthesis after "Name Not Found"))

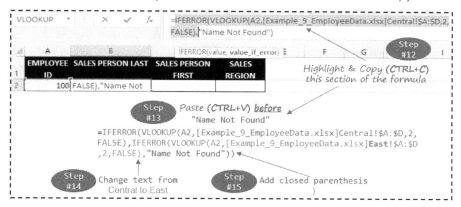

Part 2 of the **nested Vlookup formula** should be as follows, (*there are no spaces in the below*):

```
=IFERROR(VLOOKUP(A2,[Example_9_EmployeeData.xlsx]Central!$A
:$D,2,FALSE),IFERROR(VLOOKUP(A2,[Example_9_EmployeeData.xls
x]East!$A:$D,2,FALSE),"Name Not Found"))
```

16. Copy the updated IFERROR & VLOOKUP function to cells 'B3:B10'

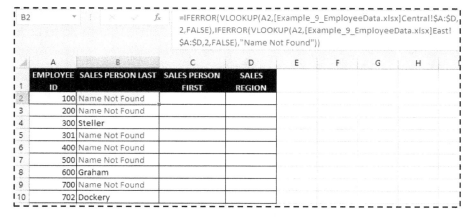

Almost done, next we'll add the final segment to our nested VLOOKUP function. This will search the *third worksheet* called **'West'** in Workbook #2 (Employee Data).

17. Return to the Example_9_**ManagersReport**.xlsx spreadsheet and select cell '**B2**'

18. Select *(highlight)* and copy (CTRL+C) this section of the formula:
    ```
    IFERROR(VLOOKUP(A2,[Example_9_EmployeeData.xlsx]East!$A
    :$D,2,FALSE),
    ```

19. **Paste (CTRL+V)** *before* `"Name Not Found"))`

20. Change the text from `East!` to `West!`

21. Add the additional parenthesis after `"Name Not Found")))`

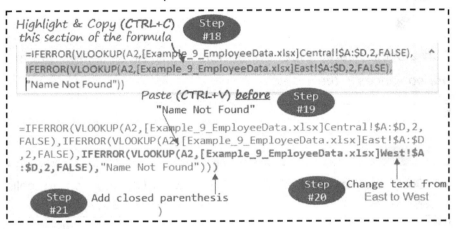

22. Copy and paste the updated nested VLOOKUP formula to cells '**B3:B10**'

| B2 | ▼ | : | × | ✓ | fx | =IFERROR(VLOOKUP(A2,[Example_9_EmployeeData.xlsx]Central!$A:$D,2,FALSE), IFERROR(VLOOKUP(A2,[Example_9_EmployeeData.xlsx]East!$A:$D,2,FALSE), IFERROR(VLOOKUP(A2,[Example_9_EmployeeData.xlsx]West!$A:$D,2,FALSE), "Name Not Found"))) |

	A	B	C	D	E	F	G	H	I
1	EMPLOYEE ID	SALES PERSON LAST	SALES PERSON FIRST	SALES REGION					
2	100	Winchester							
3	200	Graham							
4	300	Steller							
5	301	Butler							
6	400	Simpson							
7	500	Tanner							
8	600	Graham							
9	700	Danner							
10	702	Dockery							

```
=IFERROR(VLOOKUP(A2,[Example_9_EmployeeData.xlsx]Central!$A:$D,2,FALSE),
IFERROR(VLOOKUP(A2,[Example_9_EmployeeData.xlsx]East!$A:$D,2,FALSE),
IFERROR(VLOOKUP(A2,[Example_9_EmployeeData.xlsx]West!$A:$D,2,FALSE),
"Name Not Found")))
```

Great job! If you had trouble, don't worry, this was a complex nested IF VLOOKUP function. You'll get better with practice. It often still takes me a couple of tries to get the formula correct and I have had years of experience. It is very easy to miss a comma or parenthesis with these advanced functions. Your skill level will improve with repetition.

To complete the scenario, we're going to copy the formula to the columns **'SALES PERSON FIRST'** & **'REGION'** on workbook #1 (Manager's Report). Before we begin copying the IFERROR & VLOOKUP function, we need to add the **U.S. dollar $** symbol to the **Lookup_value**.

23. Return to the Example_9_ManagersReport.xlsx spreadsheet and select cell **'B2'**

24. For each Lookup_value, add the **$ before A2**

```
For cell 'B2' of the workbook
Example_9_ManagersReport.xlsx

=IFERROR(VLOOKUP($A2,[Example_9_EmployeeData.xlsx]Central!$A:$D,2,FALSE)
,IFERROR(VLOOKUP($A2,[Example_9_EmployeeData.xlsx]East!$A:$D,2,FALSE),IF
ERROR(VLOOKUP($A2,[Example_9_EmployeeData.xlsx]West!$A:$D,2,FALSE),"Name
Not Found")))
```

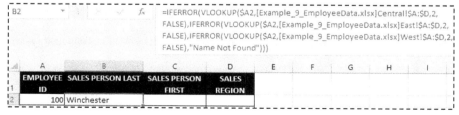

25. Copy the updated nested VLOOKUP formula to cell **'C2'**

26. In cell **'C2'** change the **Col_index_num** for all VLOOKUP formulas to **3** *(from 2)*

```
=IFERROR(VLOOKUP($A2,[Example_9_EmployeeData.xlsx]Central!$A:$D,3,FAL
SE),IFERROR(VLOOKUP($A2,[Example_9_EmployeeData.xlsx]East!$A:$D,3,FAL
SE),IFERROR(VLOOKUP($A2,[Example_9_EmployeeData.xlsx]West!$A:$D,3,FAL
SE),"Name Not Found")))
```
Step #26

27. Copy and paste the updated nested VLOOKUP formula to cells **'C3:C10'**

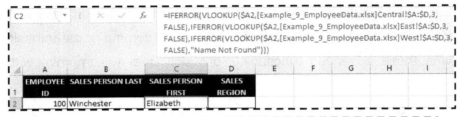

28. Copy the updated nested VLOOKUP formula to cell **'D2'**

29. Select cell **'D2'** and change the **Col_index_num** for all VLOOKUP formulas to **4**

```
=IFERROR(VLOOKUP($A2,[Example_9_EmployeeData.xlsx]Central!$A:$D,4,FAL
SE),IFERROR(VLOOKUP($A2,[Example_9_EmployeeData.xlsx]East!$A:$D,4,FAL
SE),IFERROR(VLOOKUP($A2,[Example_9_EmployeeData.xlsx]West!$A:$D,4,FAL
SE),"Name Not Found")))
```
Step #29

30. Copy and paste the updated nested VLOOKUP formula to cells **'D3:D10'**

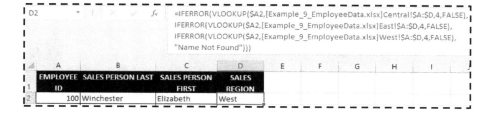

The final report should look like the following:

	A	B	C	D
1	**EMPLOYEE ID**	**SALES PERSON LAST**	**SALES PERSON FIRST**	**SALES REGION**
2	100	Winchester	Elizabeth	West
3	200	Graham	Peter	West
4	300	Steller	Alex	Central
5	301	Butler	Catherine	East
6	400	Simpson	Helen	East
7	500	Tanner	Joe	West
8	600	Graham	Maggie	Central
9	700	Danner	Peter	East
10	702	Dockery	Kevin	Central

Congratulations! You've successfully applied a VLOOKUP formula across multiple worksheets and workbooks.

Included with this exercise is a **'Completed Formula'** worksheet if needed.

You've completed the scenario. The new manager has been given a consolidated report that lists the *Sales Person ID*, *First & Last Name*, and *Region* for all of her employees.

While the VLOOKUP and associated functions are very useful and quite powerful, it can be challenging and sometimes frustrating to learn them. Why a VLOOKUP is not returning the correct value can puzzle even the most experienced users. The final chapter in this book addresses some of the more common VLOOKUP errors and how to resolve them. The areas reviewed are:

- Why am I receiving the **#N/A error message**?
- My **Lookup_value** is the same as the match value in the **Table_array**, why is my VLOOKUP formula not returning a value?
- Why am I getting the **#REF error message**?
- My VLOOKUP formula was working, but now I'm getting the wrong values, why?

Some of the below examples can be a little tricky to understand as they involve formatting issues, such as extra spaces and/or mismatched text case of the Lookup_value. However, with a little practice knowing what to look for and how to resolve these issues will save yourself hours of aggravation!

#N/A ERROR MESSAGE (EXAMPLE 1)

ERROR	Why am I receiving the **#N/A error message**?
POSSIBLE EXPLANATION	The field you want to match, the **Lookup_value**, *IS NOT* the *FIRST COLUMN* in the range of cells you specify in the **Table_array**
EXAMPLE	VLOOKUP formula appears correct, but since we're matching on the **'SALES PERSON ID'**, this column needs to be *FIRST* in the Table_array.

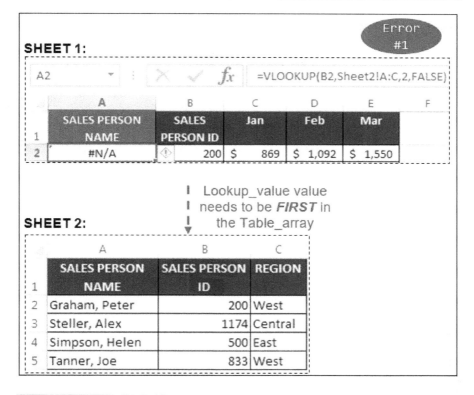

SOLUTION	Make the **'SALES PERSON ID'**, the first column in the Table_array or use the INDEX + MATCH functions.

SHEET 1:

Solution
#1

A2	▾	:	✕	✓	*fx*	=VLOOKUP(B2,Sheet2!A:C,2,FALSE)

	A	B	C	D	E	F
1	SALES PERSON NAME	SALES PERSON ID	Jan	Feb	Mar	
2	Graham, Peter	200	$ 869	$ 1,092	$ 1,550	

SHEET 2: ⌐ – – – –Corrected

	A	B	C
1	SALES PERSON ID	SALES PERSON NAME	REGION
2	200	Graham, Peter	West
3	1174	Steller, Alex	Central
4	500	Simpson, Helen	East
5	833	Tanner, Joe	West

#N/A ERROR MESSAGE (EXAMPLE 2)

ERROR	Why am I getting the **#N/A error message**? My **Lookup_value** _is_ the FIRST COLUMN in the range of cells specified in the Table_array. What else could be wrong?
POSSIBLE EXPLANATION	**Extra spaces** in the Lookup_value or Table_array
EXAMPLE	Most of the time you can't see extra spaces, especially if they are after the Lookup_value, but these invisible nuisances will cause your VLOOKUP to fail.

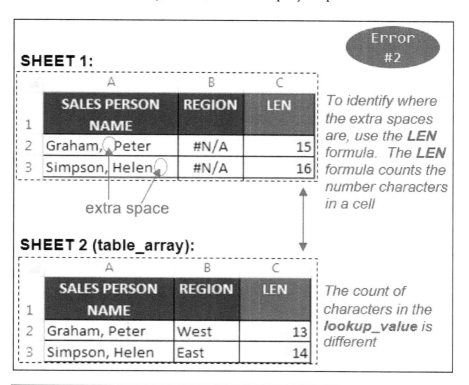

SHEET 1:

	A	B	C
1	**SALES PERSON NAME**	**REGION**	**LEN**
2	Graham, Peter	#N/A	15
3	Simpson, Helen	#N/A	16

extra space

To identify where the extra spaces are, use the **LEN** formula. The **LEN** formula counts the number characters in a cell

SHEET 2 (table_array):

	A	B	C
1	**SALES PERSON NAME**	**REGION**	**LEN**
2	Graham, Peter	West	13
3	Simpson, Helen	East	14

The count of characters in the *lookup_value* is different

SOLUTION	Identify where the extra spaces are and then remove them

Solution #2

SHEET 1:

	A	B	C
1	**SALES PERSON NAME**	**REGION**	**LEN**
2	Graham, Peter	West	13
3	Simpson, Helen	East	14

#N/A ERROR MESSAGE (EXAMPLE 3)

ERROR	What else could cause the **#N/A error message?**
POSSIBLE EXPLANATION	A similar formatting issue causing a VLOOKUP to fail is related to ***mismatched case*** of the Lookup_value.

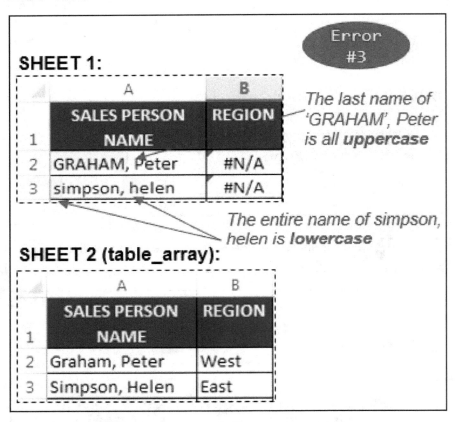

SHEET 1:

*The last name of 'GRAHAM', Peter is all **uppercase***

	A	B
	SALES PERSON NAME	**REGION**
1		
2	GRAHAM, Peter	#N/A
3	simpson, helen	#N/A

*The entire name of simpson, helen is **lowercase***

SHEET 2 (table_array):

	A	B
	SALES PERSON NAME	**REGION**
1		
2	Graham, Peter	West
3	Simpson, Helen	East

SOLUTION	Change the case formatting to match the Table_array

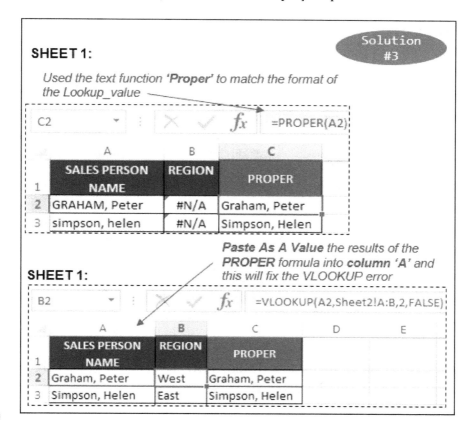

#REF ERROR MESSAGE

ERROR	Why am I getting the **#REF** error message?
POSSIBLE EXPLANATION	A common cause is the **Table_array** range of cells is incorrect.

In the example below, the VLOOKUP in sheet 1 is referencing *2 columns* in the Table_array. The **#REF error** is because the **Col_index_num** is referencing *column 3*, but that column is NOT included in the Table_array.

SHEET 1:

C2	▼	⁝	✕	✓	*fx*	=VLOOKUP($A2,Sheet2!$A:$B,3,FALSE)

	A	B	C	D	E	F
1	SALES PERSON NAME	REGION	MANAGER ID			
2	Graham, Peter	Wes⬧	#REF!			
3	Simpson, Helen	East	#REF!			

SHEET 2 (Table_array):

	A	B	C
1	Number of Columns:		
2	1	2	3
3	SALES PERSON NAME	REGION	MANAGER ID
4	Graham, Peter	West	50
5	Simpson, Helen	East	40

SOLUTION	Change the Table_array to include the correct number of columns.

SHEET 1:

C2	▼	⁝	✕	✓	*fx*	=VLOOKUP($A2,Sheet2!$A:$C,3,FALSE)

	A	B	C	D	E	F
1	SALES PERSON NAME	REGION	MANAGER ID			
2	Graham, Peter	West	50			
3	Simpson, Helen	East	40			

MY VLOOKUP FORMULA WAS WORKING, BUT NOW I'M GETTING THE WRONG VALUES, WHY?

ERROR	Why did my Vlookup stop working?
POSSIBLE EXPLANATION	Someone has inadvertently added or deleted columns in the **Table_array** range of cells

In the example below, REGION *was* being populated correctly. Let's say, you reviewed this report on a Friday, but then on the following Monday, when you opened the same report, the results were different. Why?

SHEET 1 (correct on *Friday*):

	A	B	C
	SALES PERSON NAME	REGION	MANAGER ID
1			
2	Graham, Peter	West	50
3	Simpson, Helen	East	40

SHEET 1 (incorrect on *Monday*):

	A	B	C
	SALES PERSON NAME	REGION	MANAGER ID
1			
2	Graham, Peter	100	West
3	Simpson, Helen	200	East

After reviewing the Table_array, you discover someone has added **two new columns**; 'SALES PERSON ID' and 'HOME OFFICE LOCATION'.

SHEET 2 (Table_array):

	A	B	C	D	E
	SALES PERSON NAME	SALES PERSON ID	HOME OFFICE LOCATION	REGION	MANAGER ID
1					
2	Graham, Peter	100	Seattle	West	50
3	Simpson, Helen	200	London	East	40

SOLUTION	Adjust your VLOOKUP formula to account for the newly inserted columns.

SHEET 1:

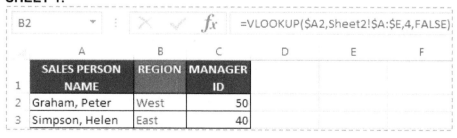

B2			fx	=VLOOKUP($A2,Sheet2!$A:$E,4,FALSE)

	A	B	C	D	E	F
1	SALES PERSON NAME	REGION	MANAGER ID			
2	Graham, Peter	West	50			
3	Simpson, Helen	East	40			

Thank you!

Your opinion?

Thank you for purchasing and reading this book, we hope you found it helpful! Your feedback is valued and appreciated! Please take a few minutes and leave a review.

MORE BOOKS AVAILABLE FROM THIS AUTHOR

For a complete list please visit us at:
https://bentonbooks.wixsite.com/bentonbooks/buy-books

- Excel Pivot Tables & Introduction To Dashboards The Step-By-Step Guide *(version 2016)*
- Excel 2016 The 30 Most Common Formulas & Features - The Step-By-Step Guide
- Excel Macros & VBA For Business Users - A Beginners Guide

QUESTIONS / FEEDBACK

Email: bentontrainingbooks@gmail.com
Website: https://bentonbooks.wixsite.com/bentonbooks

www.ingramcontent.com/pod-product-compliance
Lightning Source LLC
Chambersburg PA
CBHW061018050326
40689CB00012B/2676